BENEDICT XVI

THE MEDIEVAL FATHERS & WRITERS

The Spiritual Masters

CATHOLIC TRUTH SOCIETY
PUBLISHERS TO THE HOLY SEE

Cover credit: Andrea di Bonaiuto, *The Triumph of St Thomas Aquinas*, Santa Maria Novella, Florence
Picture credit on pages 6-7: Andrea di Bonaiuto, *Sts Peter Martyr and Thomas Aquinas confound the heretics,* detail, Spanish Chapel, Santa Maria Novella, Florence

This translated edition published in the UK 2011 by the Incorporated Catholic Truth Society, London

Printed and bound by LEGO Spa, Italy

ISBN 978-1-86082-723-5

CONTENTS

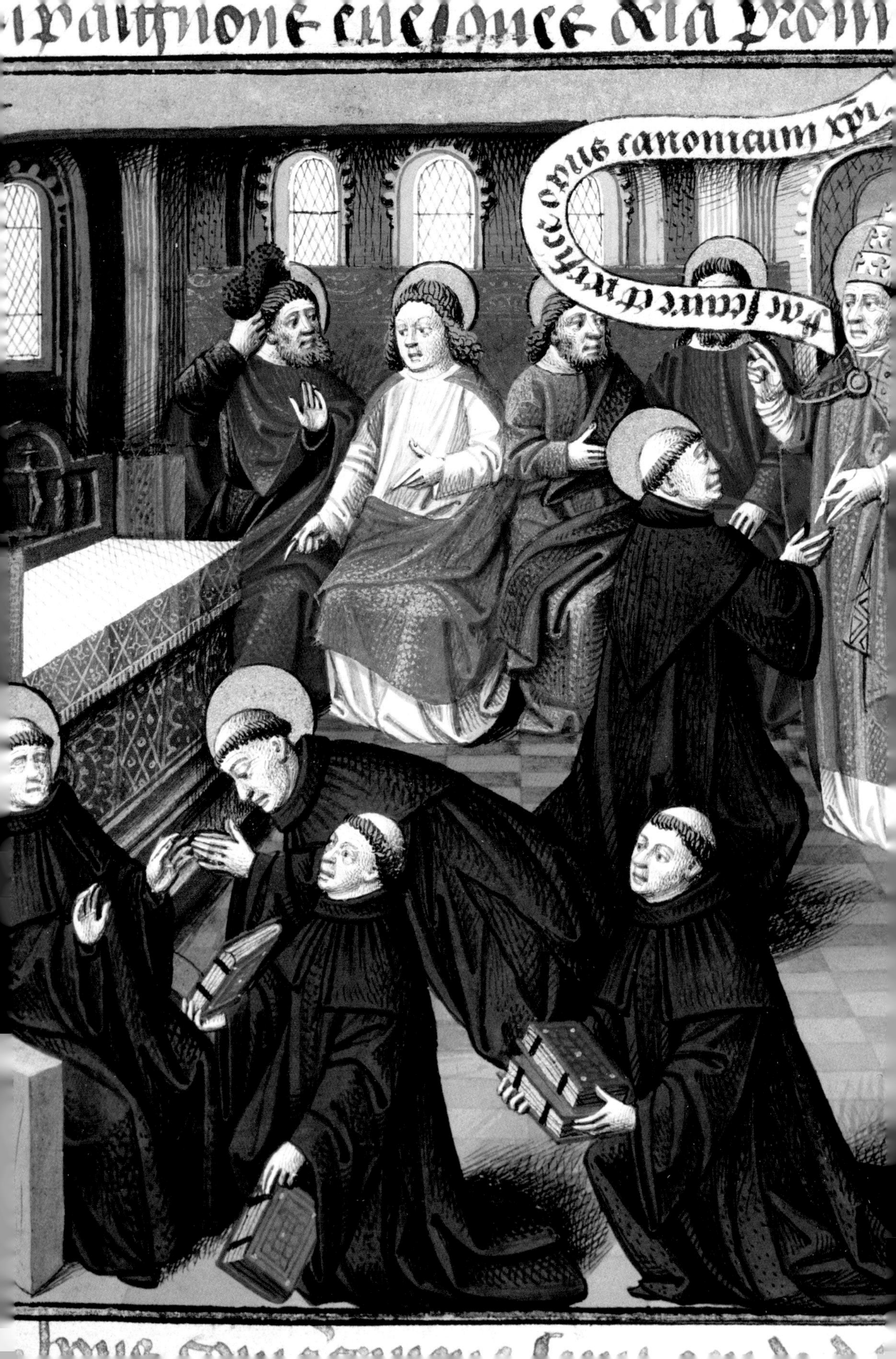

...partisione euelonce de la prom...

Fac scaire et mystice opus canonicum xpi.

Saint Odo of Cluny

After a long pause, I would like to resume the presentation of important writers of the Eastern and Western Church in the Middle Ages because in their life and writings we see as in a mirror what it means to be Christian. In this chapter we explore the luminous figure of St Odo, Abbot of Cluny. He fits into that period of medieval monasticism which saw the surprising success in Europe of the life and spirituality inspired by the *Rule of St Benedict*. In those centuries there was a wonderful increase in the number of cloisters that sprang up and branched out over the continent, spreading the Christian spirit and sensibility far and wide. St Odo takes us back in particular to Cluny, one of the most illustrious and famous monasteries in the Middle Ages that still today reveals to us, through its majestic ruins, the signs of a past rendered glorious by intense dedication to ascesis, study and, in a special way, to divine worship, endowed with decorum and beauty.

Odo was the second Abbot of Cluny. He was born in about 880, on the boundary between the Maine and the Touraine

Odo of Cluny, miniature, Ms 722/1196, fol. 124r, Musée Condé, Chantilly

regions of France. Odo's father consecrated him to the holy Bishop Martin of Tours, in whose beneficent shadow and memory he was to spend his entire life, which he ended close to St Martin's tomb. His choice of religious consecration was preceded by the inner experience of a special moment of grace, of which he himself spoke to another monk, John the Italian, who later became his biographer. Odo was still an adolescent, about 16 years old, when one Christmas Eve he felt this prayer to the Virgin rise spontaneously to his lips: "My Lady, Mother of Mercy, who on this night gave birth to the Saviour, pray for me. May your glorious and unique experience of childbirth, O Most Devout Mother, be my refuge" (*Vita sancti Odonis*, 1, 9: *PL* 133, 747). The name "Mother of Mercy", with which young Odo then invoked the Virgin, was to be the title by which he always subsequently liked to address Mary. He also called her "the one Hope of the world ... thanks to whom the gates of Heaven were opened to us" (*In veneratione S. Mariae Magdalenae: PL* 133, 721). At that time Odo chanced to come across the *Rule of St Benedict* and to comment on it, "bearing, while not yet a monk, the light yoke of monks" (*ibid.,* I, 14, *PL* 133, 50). In one of his sermons Odo was to celebrate Benedict as the "lamp that shines in the dark period of life" (*De sancto Benedicto abbate: PL* 133, 725), and to describe him as "a teacher of spiritual discipline" (*ibid., PL* 133, 727). He was to point out with affection that Christian piety, "with the liveliest gentleness commemorates him" in the knowledge that God raised him "among the supreme and elect Fathers of Holy Church" (*ibid., PL* 133, 722).

Fascinated by the Benedictine ideal, Odo left Tours and entered the Benedictine Abbey of Baume as a monk; he later moved to Cluny, of which in 927 he became abbot. From that centre of spiritual life he was able to exercise a vast influence over the monasteries on the continent. Various monasteries or coenobiums were able to benefit from his guidance and reform, including that of St Paul Outside-the-Walls. More than once Odo visited Rome and he even went as far as Subiaco, Monte Cassino and Salerno. He actually fell ill in Rome in the summer of 942. Feeling that he was nearing his end, he was determined, and made every effort, to return to St Martin in Tours, where he died, in the Octave of the Saint's feast, on 18 November 942. His biographer, stressing the "virtue of patience" that Odo possessed, gives a long list of his other virtues that include contempt of the world, zeal for souls and the commitment to peace in the Churches. Abbot Odo's great aspirations were: concord between kings and princes, the observance of the commandments, attention to the poor, the correction of youth and respect for the elderly (cf. *Vita sancti Odonis,* I, 17: *PL* 133, 49).

He loved the cell in which he dwelled, "removed from the eyes of all, eager to please God alone" (*ibid.,* I, 14: *PL* 133, 49). However, he did not fail also to exercise, as a "superabundant source", the ministry of the word and to set an example, "regretting the immense wretchedness of this world" (*ibid.,* I, 17: *PL* 133, 51). In a single monk, his biographer comments, were combined the different virtues that exist, which are found to be few and far between in other monasteries: "Jesus, in his goodness, drawing on the various gardens of monks, in a small space created a paradise, in order to water the hearts of the faithful from its fountains" (*ibid.,* I, 14: *PL* 133,49). In a passage from a sermon in honour of Mary of Magdala the Abbot of Cluny reveals to us how he conceived of monastic life: "Mary, who, seated at the Lord's feet, listened attentively to his words, is the symbol of the sweetness of contemplative life; the more its savour is tasted, the more it induces the mind to be detached from visible things and the tumult of the world's preoccupations" (*In ven. S. Mariae Magd.*, *PL* 133, 717). Odo strengthened and developed this conception in his other writings. From them transpire his love for interiority, a vision of the world as a brittle, precarious reality from which to uproot oneself, a constant inclination to detachment from things felt to be sources of anxiety, an acute sensitivity to the presence of evil in the various types of people and a deep eschatological aspiration. This vision of the world may appear rather distant from our own; yet Odo's conception of it, his perception of the fragility of the world, values an inner life that is open to the other, to the love of one's neighbour, and in this very way transforms life and opens the world to God's light.

The "devotion" to the Body and Blood of Christ which Odo in the face of a widespread neglect of them which he himself deeply deplored always cultivated with conviction deserves special mention. Odo was in fact firmly convinced of the Real Presence, under the Eucharistic species, of the Body and Blood of the Lord, by virtue of the conversion of the "substance" of the bread and the wine. He wrote: "God, Creator of all things, took the bread saying that this was his Body and that he would offer it for the world, and he distributed the wine, calling it his Blood"; now, "it is a law of nature that the change should come about in accordance with the Creator's command", and thus "nature immediately changes its usual condition: the bread instantly becomes flesh, and the wine becomes blood"; at the Lord's order, "the substance changes" (*Odonis Abb. Cluniac. occupatio,* ed. A. Swoboda, Leipzig 1900, p. 121). Unfortunately, our abbot notes, this "sacrosanct mystery of the Lord's Body, in whom the whole salvation of the world consists", (*Collationes,* XXVIII: *PL* 133, 572), is celebrated carelessly. "Priests", he

Cluny Abbey, external view

warns, "who approach the altar unworthily, stain the bread, that is, the Body of Christ" (*ibid., PL* 133, 572-573). Only those who are spiritually united to Christ may worthily participate in his Eucharistic Body: should the contrary be the case, to eat his Flesh and to drink his Blood would not be beneficial but rather a condemnation (cf. *ibid.,* XXX, *PL* 133, 575). All this invites us to believe the truth of the Lord's presence with new force and depth. The presence in our midst of the Creator, who gives himself into our hands and transforms us as he transforms the bread and the wine, thus transforms the world.

St Odo was a true spiritual guide both for the monks and for the faithful of his time. In the face of the "immensity of the vices widespread in society, the remedy he strongly advised was that of a radical change of life, based on humility, austerity, detachment from ephemeral things and adherence to those that are eternal (cf. *Collationes*, *XXX*, *PL* 133, 613). In spite of the realism of his diagnosis on the situation of his time, Odo does not indulge in pessimism: "We do not say this", he explains, "in order to plunge those who wish to convert into despair. Divine mercy is always available; it awaits the hour of our conversion" (*ibid., PL* 133, 563). And he exclaims: "O ineffable bowels of divine piety! God pursues wrongs and yet protects sinners" (*ibid., PL* 133, 592). Sustained by this conviction, the Abbot of Cluny used to like to pause to contemplate the mercy of Christ, the Saviour whom he describes evocatively as "a lover of men": *"amator hominum Christus"* (*ibid.,* LIII: *PL* 133, 637). He observes "Jesus took upon himself the scourging that would have been our due in order to save the creature he formed and loves (cf. *ibid., PL* 133, 638).

Here, a trait of the holy abbot appears that at first sight is almost hidden beneath the rigour of his austerity as a reformer: his deep, heartfelt kindness. He was austere, but above all he was good, a man of great goodness, a goodness that comes from contact with the divine goodness. Thus Odo, his peers tell us, spread around him his overflowing joy. His biographer testifies that he never heard "such mellifluous words" on human lips (*ibid.,* I, 17: *PL* 133, 31). His biographer also records that he was in the habit of asking the children he met along the way to sing, and that he would then give them some small token, and he adds: "Abbot Odo's words were full of joy ... his merriment instilled in our hearts deep joy" (*ibid.,* II, 5: *PL* 133, 63). In this way the energetic yet at the same time lovable medieval abbot, enthusiastic about reform, with incisive action nourished in his monks, as well as in the lay faithful of his time, the resolution to progress swiftly on the path of Christian perfection.

Let us hope that his goodness, the joy that comes from faith, together with austerity and opposition to the world's vices, may also move our hearts, so that we too may find the source of the joy that flows from God's goodness.

Saint Peter Damian

Let us now reflect on one of the most significant figures of the 11th century. St Peter Damian, a monk, a lover of solitude and at the same time a fearless man of the Church, committed personally to the task of reform, initiated by the Popes of the time. He was born in Ravenna in 1007, into a noble family but in straitened circumstances. He was left an orphan and his childhood was not exempt from hardships and suffering, although his sister Roselinda tried to be a mother to him and his elder brother, Damian, adopted him as his son. For this very reason he was to be called Piero di Damiano, Pier Damiani [Peter of Damian, Peter Damian]. He was educated first at Faenza and then at Parma where, already at the age of 25, we find him involved in teaching. As well as a good grounding in the field of law, he acquired a refined expertise in the art of writing the *ars scribendi* and, thanks to his knowledge of the great Latin classics, became "one of the most accomplished Latinists of his time, one of the greatest writers of medieval Latin" (J. Leclercq, *Pierre Damien, ermite et homme d'Église,* Rome, 1960, p. 172).

Master of Peter Damian, *St Peter Damian,* Museo d'arte, Ravenna

He distinguished himself in the widest range of literary forms: from letters to sermons, from hagiographies to prayers, from poems to epigrams. His sensitivity to beauty led him to poetic contemplation of the world. Peter Damian conceived of the universe as a never-ending "parable" and a sequence of symbols on which to base the interpretation of inner life and divine and supra-natural reality. In this perspective, in about the year 1034, contemplation of the absolute of God impelled him gradually to detach himself from the world and from its transient realties and to withdraw to the Monastery of Fonte Avellana. It had been founded only a few decades earlier but was already celebrated for its austerity. For the monks' edification he wrote the Life of the Founder, St Romuald of Ravenna, and at the same time strove to deepen their spirituality, expounding on his ideal of eremitic monasticism.

One detail should be immediately emphasised: the Hermitage at Fonte Avellana was dedicated to the Holy Cross and the Cross was the Christian mystery that was to fascinate Peter Damian more than all the others. "Those who do not love the Cross of Christ do not love Christ", he said (*Sermo XVIII*, 11, p. 117); and he described himself as "*Petrus crucis Christi servorum famulus* Peter, servant of the servants of the Cross of Christ" (*Ep* 9, 1). Peter Damian addressed the most beautiful prayers to the Cross in which he reveals a vision of this mystery which has cosmic dimensions for it embraces the entire history of salvation: "O Blessed Cross", he exclaimed, "You are venerated, preached and honoured by the faith of the Patriarchs, the predictions of the Prophets, the senate that judges the Apostles, the victorious army of Martyrs and the throngs of all the Saints" (*Sermo XLVII*, 14, p. 304). Dear Brothers and Sisters, may the example of St Peter Damian spur us too always to look to the Cross as to the supreme act God's love for humankind of God, who has given us salvation.

This great monk compiled a Rule for eremitical life in which he heavily stressed the "rigour of the hermit": in the silence of the cloister the monk is called to spend a life of prayer, by day and by night, with prolonged and strict fasting; he must put into practice generous brotherly charity in ever prompt and willing obedience to the prior. In study and in the daily meditation of Sacred Scripture, Peter Damian discovered the mystical meaning of the word of God, finding in it nourishment for his spiritual life. In this regard he described the hermit's cell as the "parlour in which God converses with men". For him, living as a hermit was the peak of Christian existence, "the loftiest of the states of life" because the monk, now free from the bonds of worldly life and of his own self, receives "a dowry from the Holy Spirit and his happy soul is united with its heavenly Spouse" (*Ep* 18, 17; cf. *Ep* 28, 43 ff.). This is important for us today too, even though we are not monks: to know how to make silence within us to listen to God's voice, to seek, as it were, a "parlour" in which God speaks with us: learning the word of God in prayer and in meditation is the path to life.

St Peter Damian, who was essentially a man of prayer, meditation and contemplation, was also a fine theologian: his reflection on various doctrinal themes led him to important conclusions for life. Thus, for example, he expresses with clarity and liveliness the Trinitarian doctrine, already using, under the guidance of biblical and patristic texts, the three fundamental terms which were subsequently to become crucial also for the philosophy of the West: *processio, relatio* and *persona* (cf. *Opusc. XXXVIII*: *PL* CXLV, 633-642; and *Opusc.* II and III: *ibid.,* 41 ff. and 58 ff). However, because

si che tosto couien chessi riueli
In quelloco fuio pietro damiano
et pietro puscator fu nela casa
di nostra dōna in sullito adriano
Poca uita mortal mera rimasa
quandio fui chesto et tracto aquel cappello
ke pur dimale impegio si trauasa
Venne cephas et uēne il gran uasello
delo spō scō macri et scalzi
prendendo ilcibo da qualūq; hostello
Or uollion quinci et quindi chi rincalzi
li moderni pastori et chili meni
tanto son graui et chi diretro lialzi
Cuopron dimanti loro ipalafreni
siche due bestie uan soctuna pelle
opatientia che tanto sostieni

theological analysis of the mystery led him to contemplate the intimate life of God and the dialogue of ineffable love between the three divine Persons, he drew ascetic conclusions from them for community life and even for relations between Latin and Greek Christians, divided on this topic. His meditation on the figure of Christ is significantly reflected in practical life, since the whole of Scripture is centred on him. The "Jews", St Peter Damian notes, "through the pages of Sacred Scripture, bore Christ on their shoulders as it were" (*Sermo XLVI*, 15). Therefore Christ, he adds, must be the centre of the monk's life: "May Christ be heard in our language, may Christ be seen in our life, may he be perceived in our hearts" (*Sermo VIII*, 5). Intimate union with Christ engages not only monks but all the baptised. Here we find a strong appeal for us too not to let ourselves be totally absorbed by the activities, problems and preoccupations of every day, forgetting that Jesus must truly be the centre of our life.

Communion with Christ creates among Christians a unity of love. In Letter 28, which is a brilliant ecclesiological treatise, Peter Damian develops a profound theology of the Church as communion. "Christ's Church", he writes, is united by the bond of charity to the point that just as she has many members so is she, mystically, entirely contained in a single member; in such a way that the whole universal Church is rightly called the one Bride of Christ in the singular, and each chosen soul, through the sacramental mystery, is considered fully Church". This is important: not only that the whole universal Church should be united, but that the Church should be present in her totality in each one of us. Thus the service of the individual becomes "an

Scenes from the life of St Peter Damian, miniature, *Divine Comedy* by Dante Alighieri, Ms Yates Thompson 36, fol. 167r, British Library, London

expression of universality" (*Ep* 28, 9-23). However, the ideal image of "Holy Church" illustrated by Peter Damian does not correspond as he knew well to the reality of his time. For this reason he did not fear to denounce the state of corruption that existed in the monasteries and among the clergy, because, above all, of the practice of the conferral by the lay authorities of ecclesiastical offices; various Bishops and Abbots were behaving as the rulers of their subjects rather than as pastors of souls. Their moral life frequently left much to be desired. For this reason, in 1057 Peter Damian left his monastery with great reluctance and sorrow and accepted, if unwillingly, his appointment as Cardinal Bishop of Ostia. So it was that he entered fully into collaboration with the Popes in the difficult task of Church reform. He saw that to make his own contribution of helping in the work of the Church's renewal contemplation did not suffice. He thus relinquished the beauty of the hermitage and courageously undertook numerous journeys and missions.

Because of his love for monastic life, 10 years later, in 1067, he obtained permission to return to Fonte Avellana and resigned from the Diocese of Ostia. However, the tranquillity he had longed for did not last long: two years later, he was sent to Frankfurt in an endeavour to prevent the divorce of Henry IV from his wife Bertha. And again, two years later, in 1071, he went to Monte Cassino for the consecration of the abbey church and at the beginning of 1072, to Ravenna, to re-establish peace with the local Archbishop who had supported the antipope bringing interdiction upon the city. On the journey home to his hermitage, an unexpected illness obliged him to stop at the Benedictine Monastery of Santa Maria Vecchia Fuori Porta in Faenza, where he died in the night between 22 and 23 February 1072.

It is a great grace that the Lord should have raised up in the life of the Church a figure as exuberant, rich and complex as St Peter Damian. Moreover, it is rare to find theological works and spirituality as keen and vibrant as those of the Hermitage at Fonte Avellana. St Peter Damian was a monk through and through, with forms of austerity which to us today might even seem excessive. Yet, in that way he made monastic life an eloquent testimony of God's primacy and an appeal to all to walk towards holiness, free from any compromise with evil. He spent himself, with lucid consistency and great severity, for the reform of the Church of his time. He gave all his spiritual and physical energies to Christ and to the Church, but always remained, as he liked to describe himself, *Petrus ultimus monachorum servus*, Peter, the lowliest servant of the monks.

Symeon the New Theologian

Now I should like to reflect on an Eastern monk, Symeon the New Theologian, whose writings have had a notable influence on the theology and spirituality of the East, in particular with regard to the experience of mystical union with God. Symeon the New Theologian was born in 949 in Galatai, Paphlagonia, in Asia Minor, into a provincial noble family. While he was still young he moved to Constantinople to complete his education and enter the Emperor's service. However, he did not feel attracted by the civil career that awaited him. Under the influence of the inner illumination he was experiencing, he set out in search of someone who would guide him in the period of doubt and perplexity he was living through and help him advance on the path of union with God. He found this spiritual guide in Symeon the Pious (*Eulabes*), a simple monk of the *Studios* in Constantinople who advised him to read Mark the Monk's treatise, *The Spiritual Law*. Symeon the New Theologian found in this text a teaching that made a deep impression on him: "If you seek spiritual healing, be attentive to your conscience," and he read in to it: "Do all that

St Symeon, Cathedral of the Dormition in the Kremlin, detail of fresco from Altar screen it tells you and you will find what serves you". From that very moment, he himself says, he never went to sleep without first asking himself whether his conscience had anything with which to reproach him.

Symeon entered the Studite monastery where, however, his mystical experiences and extraordinary devotion to his spiritual father caused him some difficulty. He moved to the small convent of *St Mamas*, also in Constantinople, of which three years later he became abbot, *hegumen*. There he embarked on an intense quest for spiritual union with Christ which gave him great authority. It is interesting to note that he was given the title of the "New Theologian", in spite of the tradition that reserved this title for two figures, John the Evangelist and Gregory of Nazianzus. Symeon suffered misunderstandings and exile but was rehabilitated by Patriarch Sergius II of Constantinople.

Symeon the New Theologian spent the last stage of his life at the Monastery of St Marina where he wrote a large part of his opus, becoming ever more famous for his teaching and his miracles. He died on 12 March 1022.

The best known of his disciples, Niceta Stethatos, who collected and copied Symeon's writings, compiled a posthumous edition of them and subsequently wrote his biography. Symeon's opus consists of nine volumes that are divided into *theological, gnostic and practical chapters*, three books of *catecheses addressed to monks*, two books of *theological and ethical treatises* and one of *hymns*. Moreover, his numerous *Letters* should not be forgotten. All these works have had an important place in the Eastern monastic tradition to our day.

Symeon focused his reflection on the Holy Spirit's presence in the baptised and on the awareness they must have of this spiritual reality. "Christian life", he emphasised, "is intimate, personal communion with God, divine grace illumines the believer's heart and leads him to a mystical vision of the Lord". Along these lines, Symeon the New Theologian insisted that true knowledge of God does not come from books but rather from spiritual experience, from spiritual life. Knowledge of God is born from a process of inner purification that begins with conversion of heart through the power of faith and love. It passes through profound repentance and sincere sorrow for one's sins to attain union with Christ, the source of joy and peace, suffused with the light of his presence within us. For Symeon this experience of divine grace did not constitute an exceptional gift for a few mystics but rather was the fruit of Baptism in the life of every seriously committed believer.

A point on which to reflect, dear brothers and sisters! This holy Eastern monk calls us all to pay attention to our spiritual life, to the hidden presence of God within us, to the sincerity of the conscience and to purification, to conversion of heart, so that the Holy Spirit may really become present in us and guide us. Indeed, if rightly we are concerned to care for our physical, human and intellectual development, it is even more important not to neglect our inner growth. This consists in the knowledge of God, in true knowledge, not only learned from books but from within and in communion with God, to experience his help at every moment and in every circumstance. Basically it is this that Symeon describes when he recounts his own mystical experience. Already as a young man, before entering the monastery, while at home one night immersed in prayer and invoking God's help to fight temptations, he saw the room fill with light. Later, when he entered the monastery, he was given spiritual books for instruction but reading them did not procure for him the peace that he sought. He felt, he himself says, as if he were a poor little bird without wings. He humbly accepted this situation without rebelling and it was then that his visions of light began once again to increase. Wishing to assure himself of their authenticity, Symeon asked Christ directly: "Lord, is it truly you who are here?". He heard the affirmative answer resonating in his heart and was supremely comforted. "That, Lord", he was to write later, "was the first time that you considered me, a prodigal son, worthy of hearing your voice". However, not even this revelation left him entirely at peace. He wondered, rather, whether he ought to consider that experience an illusion. At last, one day an event occurred that was crucial to his mystical experience. He began to feel like "a poor man who loves his brethren" (*ptochós philádelphos*). Around him he saw hordes of enemies bent on ensnaring him and doing him harm, yet he felt within an intense surge of love for them. How can this be explained? Obviously, such great love could not come from within him but must well up from another source. Symeon realised that it was coming from Christ present within him and everything became clear: he had a sure proof that the source of love in him was Christ's presence. He was certain that having in ourselves a love that exceeds our personal intentions suggests that the source of love is in us. Thus we can say on the one hand that if we are without a certain openness to love Christ does not enter us, and on the other, that Christ becomes a source of love and transforms us. Dear friends, this experience remains particularly important for us today if we are to find the criteria that tell us whether we are truly close to God, whether God exists and dwells in us. God's love develops in us if we stay united to him with prayer and with listening to his word, with an open heart. Divine love alone prompts us to open our hearts to others and makes us sensitive to their needs, bringing us to consider everyone as brothers and sisters and inviting us to respond to hatred with love and to offence with forgiveness.

In thinking about this figure of Symeon the New Theologian, we may note a further element of his spirituality. On the path of ascetic life which he proposed and took, the monk's intense attention and concentration on the inner experience conferred an essential importance on the spiritual father of the monastery. The same young Symeon, as has been said, had found a spiritual director who gave him substantial help and whom he continued to hold in the greatest esteem such as to profess veneration for him, even in public, after his death. And I would like to say that the invitation to have recourse to a good spiritual father who can guide every individual to profound knowledge of himself and lead him to union with the Lord so that his life may be in ever closer conformity with the Gospel still applies for all priests, consecrated and lay people, and especially youth. To go towards the Lord we always need a guide, a dialogue. We cannot do it with our thoughts alone. And this is also the meaning of the ecclesiality of our faith, of finding this guide.

To conclude, we may sum up the teaching and mystical experience of Symeon the New Theologian in these words: in his ceaseless quest for God, even amidst the difficulties he encountered and the criticism of which he was the object, in the end he let himself be guided by love. He himself was able to live and teach his monks that for every disciple of Jesus the essential is to grow in love; thus we grow in the knowledge of Christ himself, to be able to say with St Paul: "It is no longer I who live, but Christ who lives in me" (*Gal* 2: 20).

Saint Anselm

The Benedictine Abbey of Sant'Anselmo [St Anselm] is located on the Aventine Hill in Rome. As the headquarters of an academic institute of higher studies and of the Abbot Primate of the Confederated Benedictines it is a place that unites within it prayer, study and governance, the same three activities that were a feature of the life of the Saint to whom it is dedicated: Anselm of Aosta, the ninth anniversary of whose death occurs this year. The many initiatives promoted for this happy event, especially by the Diocese of Aosta, have highlighted the interest that this medieval thinker continues to rouse. He is also known as Anselm of Bec and Anselm of Canterbury because of the cities with which he was associated. Who is this figure to whom three places, distant from one another and located in three different nations – Italy, France, England, – feel particularly bound? A monk with an intense spiritual life, an excellent teacher of the young, a theologian with an extraordinary capacity for speculation, a wise man of governance and an intransigent defender of *libertas Ecclesiae*, of the Church's freedom, Anselm is one of the eminent figures of the Middle Ages who was able to harmonise all these qualities, thanks to the profound mystical experience that always guided his thought and his action.

Anselm of Canterbury, engraving from a drawing by André Thévet

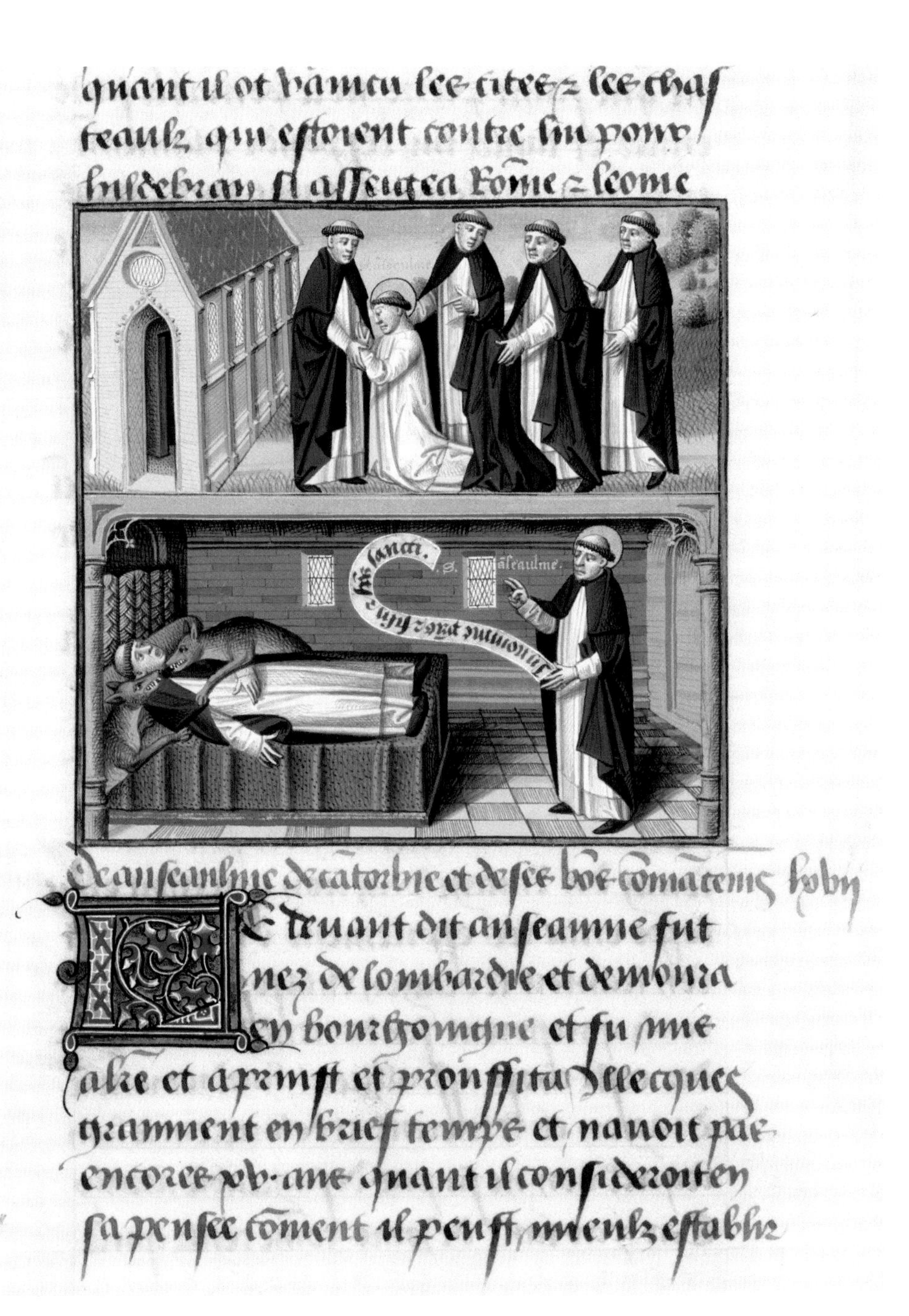

Scene from the life of Anselm of Canterbury, Ms 722, fol. 170v, miniature from *Le Miroir Historia* by Vincent de Beauvais, Musée Condé, Chantilly

St Anselm was born in 1033 (or at the beginning of 1034) in Aosta, the first child of a noble family. His father was a coarse man dedicated to the pleasures of life who squandered his possessions. On the other hand, Anselm's mother was a profoundly religious woman of high moral standing (cf. Eadmer, *Vita Sancti Anselmi*, *PL* 159, col. 49). It was she, his mother, who saw to the first human and religious formation of her son whom she subsequently entrusted to the Benedictines at a priory in Aosta. Anselm, who since childhood as his biographer recounts imagined that the good Lord dwelled among the towering, snow-capped peaks of the Alps, dreamed one night that he had been invited to this splendid kingdom by God himself, who had a long and affable conversation with him and then gave him to eat "a very white bread roll" (*ibid.,* col. 51). This dream left him with the conviction that he was called to carry out a lofty mission. At the age of 15, he asked to be admitted to the Benedictine Order but his father brought the full force of his authority to bear against him and did not even give way when his son, seriously ill and feeling close to death, begged for the religious habit as a supreme comfort. After his recovery and the premature death of his mother, Anselm went through a period of moral dissipation. He neglected his studies and, consumed by earthly passions, grew deaf to God's call. He left home and began to wander through France in search of new experiences. Three years later, having arrived in Normandy, he went to the Benedictine Abbey of Bec, attracted by the fame of Lanfranc of Pavia, the Prior. For him this was a providential meeting, crucial to the rest of his life. Under Lanfranc's guidance Anselm energetically resumed his studies and it was not long before he became not only the favourite pupil but also the teacher's confidante. His monastic vocation was rekindled and, after an attentive evaluation, at the age of 27 he entered the monastic order and was ordained a priest. Ascesis and study unfolded new horizons before him, enabling him to rediscover at a far higher level the same familiarity with God which he had had as a child.

When Lanfranc became Abbot of Caen in 1063, Anselm, after barely three years of monastic life, was named Prior of the Monastery of Bec and teacher of the cloister school, showing his gifts as a refined educator. He was not keen on authoritarian methods; he compared young people to small plants that develop better if they are not enclosed in greenhouses and granted them a "healthy" freedom. He was very demanding with himself and with others in monastic observance, but rather than imposing his discipline he strove to have it followed by persuasion. Upon the death of Abbot Herluin, the founder of the Abbey of Bec, Anselm was unanimously elected to succeed him; it was February 1079. In the meantime numerous monks had been summoned to Canterbury to bring to their brethren on the other side of the Channel the renewal that was being brought about on the continent. Their work was so well received that Lanfranc of Pavia, Abbot of Caen, became the new Archbishop of Canterbury. He asked Anselm to spend a certain period with him in order to instruct the monks and to help him in the difficult plight in which his ecclesiastical community had been left after the Norman conquest. Anselm's stay turned out to be very fruitful; he won such popularity and esteem that when Lanfranc died he was chosen to succeed him in the archiepiscopal See of Canterbury. He received his solemn episcopal consecration in December 1093.

Anselm immediately became involved in a strenuous struggle for the Church's freedom, valiantly supporting the independence of the spiritual power from the temporal. Anselm defended the Church from undue interference by political authorities,

Pier Francesco Foschi, *Dispute on the Immaculate Conception,*
Santo Spirito, Florence

ECCE RVBVS
ARDENS
FORMA

especially King William Rufus and Henry I, finding encouragement and support in the Roman Pontiff to whom he always showed courageous and cordial adherence. In 1103, this fidelity even cost him the bitterness of exile from his See of Canterbury. Moreover, it was only in 1106, when King Henry I renounced his right to the conferral of ecclesiastical offices, as well as to the collection of taxes and the confiscation of Church properties, that Anselm could return to England, where he was festively welcomed by the clergy and the people. Thus the long battle he had fought with the weapons of perseverance, pride and goodness ended happily. This holy Archbishop, who roused such deep admiration around him wherever he went, dedicated the last years of his life to the moral formation of the clergy and to intellectual research into theological topics. He died on 21 April 1109, accompanied by the words of the Gospel proclaimed in Holy Mass on that day: "You are those who have continued with me in my trials; as my Father appointed a kingdom for me, so do I appoint for you that you may eat and drink at my table in my kingdom..." (*Lk* 22: 28-30). So it was that the dream of the mysterious banquet he had had as a small boy, at the very beginning of his spiritual journey, found fulfilment. Jesus, who had invited him to sit at his table, welcomed Anselm upon his death into the eternal Kingdom of the Father.

"I pray, O God, to know you, to love you, that I may rejoice in you. And if I cannot attain to full joy in this life may I at least advance from day to day, until that joy shall come to the full" (*Proslogion,* chapter 14). This prayer enables us to understand the mystical soul of this great Saint of the Middle Ages, the founder of scholastic theology, to whom Christian tradition has given the title: "Magnificent Doctor", because he fostered an intense desire to deepen his knowledge of the divine Mysteries but in the full awareness that the quest for God is never ending, at least on this earth. The clarity and logical rigour of his thought always aimed at "raising the mind to contemplation of God" (*ibid., Proemium*). He states clearly that whoever intends to study theology cannot rely on his intelligence alone but must cultivate at the same time a profound experience of faith. The theologian's activity, according to St Anselm, thus develops in three stages: faith, a gift God freely offers, to be received with humility; *experience*, which consists in incarnating God's word in one's own daily life; and therefore true *knowledge*, which is never the fruit of ascetic reasoning but rather of contemplative intuition. In this regard his famous words remain more useful than ever, even today, for healthy theological research and for anyone who wishes to deepen his knowledge of the truths of faith: "I do not endeavour, O Lord, to penetrate your sublimity, for in no wise do I compare my understanding with that; but I long to understand in some degree your truth, which my heart believes and loves. For I do not seek to understand that I may believe, but I believe in order to understand. For this also I believe, that unless I believed, I should not understand" (*ibid.,* 1).

May the love of the truth and the constant thirst for God that marked St Anselm's entire existence be an incentive to every Christian to seek tirelessly an ever more intimate union with Christ, the Way, the Truth and the Life. In addition, may the zeal full of courage that distinguished his pastoral action and occasionally brought him misunderstanding, sorrow and even exile be an encouragement for Pastors, for consecrated people and for all the faithful to love Christ's Church, to pray, to work and to suffer for her, without ever abandoning or betraying her. May the Virgin Mother of God, for whom St Anselm had a tender, filial devotion, obtain this grace for us. "Mary, it is you whom my heart yearns to love", St Anselm wrote, "it is you whom my tongue ardently desires to praise".

Peter the Venerable

Peter the Venerable takes us back to the famous Abbey of Cluny, to its *decor* (decorum) and *nitor* (clarity) to use terms that recur in the Cluny texts a decorum and splendour that were admired especially in the beauty of the liturgy, a privileged way for reaching God. Even more than these aspects, however, Peter's personality recalls the holiness of the great abbots of Cluny: in Cluny "there was not a single abbot who was not a saint", Pope Gregory VII said in 1080. These holy men include Peter the Venerable who possessed more or less all the virtues of his predecessors although, under him, in comparison with the new Orders such as *Cîteaux*, Cluny began to feel some symptoms of crisis. Peter is a wonderful example of an ascetic strict with himself and understanding of others. He was born in about 1094 in the French region of Auvergne, he entered the Monastery of Sauxillanges as a child and became a monk there and then prior. In 1122 he was elected Abbot of Cluny and remained in this office until he died, on Christmas

Peter the Venerable praying before the Virgin Mary, miniature, fol. 23r, *Receuil liturgique et historique concernant Cluny*, Bibliothèque nationale de France

day 1156, as he had wished. "A lover of peace", his biographer Rudolph wrote, "he obtained peace in the glory of God on the day of peace" (*Vita*, I, 17; *PL* 189, 28)

All who knew him praised his refined meekness, his serene equilibrium, rectitude, loyalty, reasonableness and his special approach to mediation. "It is in my nature" he wrote, "to be particularly inclined to indulgence; I am urged to this by my habit of forgiveness. I am accustomed to toleration and forgiveness" (*Ep.* 192, in: *The Letters of Peter the Venerable*, Harvard University Press, 1967, p. 446). He said further: "With those who hate peace let us always seek to be peacemakers" (*Ep.* 100, *loc. cit.,* p. 261). And he wrote of himself: "I am not the type who is discontented with his lot... whose mind is always tormented by anxiety or doubt and who complains that everyone else is resting while they are the only ones working" (*Ep.* 182, p. 425). With a sensitive and affectionate nature, he could combine love for the Lord with tenderness to his family members, especially his mother, and to his friends. He cultivated friendship, especially with his monks who used to confide in him, certain that they would be heard and understood. According to his biographer's testimony: "he did not look down on anyone and never turned anyone away" (*Vita,* 1, 3: *PL* 189, 19); "he appeared friendly to all; in his innate goodness he was open to all" (*ibid.,* 1,1: *PL.* 189, 17).

We could say that this holy Abbot also sets an example to the monks and Christians of our day, marked by a frenetic pace, when episodes of intolerance, incommunicability, division and conflict are common. His testimony invites us to be able to combine love of God with love of neighbour and not to tire of building relations of brotherhood and reconciliation. Effectively Peter the Venerable acted in this way. He found himself in charge of the Monastery of Cluny in years that were far from tranquil for various reasons, both within the Abbey and outside it, and managed to be at the same time both strict and profoundly human. He used to say: "One may obtain more from a man by tolerating him than by irritating him with reproach" (*Ep.* 172, *loc. cit.,* p. 409). By virtue of his office he had to undertake frequent journeys to Italy, England, Germany and Spain. He found it hard to be wrenched from the quiet of contemplation. He confessed: "I go from one place to the next, I hurry, I am anxious, I am tormented, dragged here and there: my mind now on my own affairs and now on those of others, not without great mental agitation" (*Ep.* 91, *loc. cit.,* p. 233). Although he was obliged to navigate between the powers and nobles who surrounded Cluny, he succeeded in preserving his habitual calm, thanks to his sense of measure, magnanimity and realism. Among the important figures with whom he came into contact was Bernard of Clairvaux with whom he maintained a relationship of increasing friendship, despite the differences of their temperaments and approaches. Bernard described him as: "an important man, occupied with important affairs" and held him in high esteem (*Ep.* 147, ed. *Scriptorium Claravallense*, Milan 1986, VI/1, pp. 658-660), while Peter the Venerable described Bernard as a "lamp of the Church" (Ep 164, p. 396), and a "strong and splendid pillar of the monastic order and of the whole Church" (*Ep.* 175, p. 418).

With a lively sense of Church, Peter the Venerable affirmed that the vicissitudes of the Christian people must be felt in the "depths of the heart" by those who will be numbered "among the members of Christ's Body" (*Ep.* 164, *ibid.,* p. 397). And he added: "those who do not smart from the wounds of Christ's body are not nourished by the Spirit of Christ", wherever they may be produced (*ibid.*). In addition, he also showed care and concern for people outside the Church, in particular Jews and Muslims: to increase knowledge of the latter he provided for the translation of the Qur'an. A historian recently remarked on this subject: "In the midst of the intransigence of medieval people, even the greatest among them, we admire here a sublime example of the sensitivity to which Christian charity leads" (J. Leclercq, *Pietro il Venerabile,* Jaca Book, 1991, p. 189). Other aspects of Christian life dear to him were love for the Eucharist and devotion to the Virgin Mary. On the Blessed Sacrament he has left passages that constitute "one of the masterpieces of Eucharistic literature of all time" (*ibid.,* p. 267) and on the Mother of God he wrote illuminating reflections, contemplating her ever closely related to Jesus the Redeemer and his work of salvation. It suffices to present his inspired prayer: "Hail, Blessed Virgin, who put execration to flight. Hail, Mother of the Most High, Bride of the meekest Lamb. You have defeated the serpent, you crushed its head, when the God you bore destroyed it.... Shining Star of the East who dispelled the shadows of the west. Dawn who precedes the sun, day that knows no night.... Pray God who was born of you to dissolve our sin and, after pardoning it, to grant us his grace and his glory" (*Carmina, PL* 189, 1018-1019).

Peter the Venerable also had a predilection for literary activity and a gift for it. He noted his reflections, persuaded of the importance of using the pen as if it were a plough, "to scatter the seed of the Word on paper" (*Ep.* 20, p. 38). Although he was not a systematic theologian, he was a great investigator of God's mystery. His theology is rooted in prayer, especially in liturgical prayer, and among the mysteries of Christ he preferred the Transfiguration which prefigures the Resurrection. It was Peter himself who introduced this feast at Cluny, composing a special office for it that mirrors the characteristic theological devotion of Peter and of the Cluniac Order, which was focused entirely on contemplation of the glorious Face (*gloriosa facies*) of Christ, finding in it the reasons for that ardent joy which marked his spirit and shone out in the monastery's liturgy.

This holy monk is certainly a great example of monastic holiness, nourished from the sources of the Benedictine tradition. For him, the ideal of the monk consists in "adhering tenaciously to Christ" (*Ep.* 53, *loc. cit.,* p. 161), in a cloistered life distinguished by "monastic humility" (*ibid.*) and hard work (*Ep.* 77, *loc. cit.,* p. 211) as well as an atmosphere of silent contemplation and constant praise of God. The first and most important occupation of the monk, according to Peter of Cluny, is the solemn celebration of the Divine Office "a heavenly action and the most useful of all" (*Statutes*, I, 1026) to be accompanied by reading, meditation, personal prayer and penance observed with discretion (cf. *Ep.* 20, *loc. cit.,* p. 40). In this way the whole of life is pervaded by profound love of God and love of others, a love that is expressed in sincere openness to neighbour, in forgiveness and in the quest for peace. We might say, to conclude, that if this lifestyle, combined with daily work, was the monk's ideal for St Benedict, it also concerns all of us and can be to a large extent the lifestyle of the Christian who wants to become an authentic disciple of Christ, characterised precisely by tenacious adherence to him and by humility, diligence and the capacity for forgiveness and peace.

Saint Bernard of Clairvaux

St Bernard of Clairvaux was called "the last of the Fathers" of the Church because once again in the 12th century he renewed and brought to the fore the important theology of the Fathers. We do not know in any detail about the years of his childhood; however, we know that he was born in 1090 in Fontaines, France, into a large and fairly well-to-do family. As a very young man he devoted himself to the study of the so-called liberal arts especially grammar, rhetoric and dialectics at the school of the canons of the Church of Saint-Vorles at Châtillon-sur-Seine; and the decision to enter religious life slowly matured within him. At the age of about 20, he entered Cîteaux, a new monastic foundation that was more flexible in comparison with the ancient and venerable monasteries of the period while at the same time stricter in the practice of the evangelical counsels. A few years later, in 1115, Bernard was sent by Stephen Harding, the third Abbot of Cîteaux, to found the monastery of Clairvaux. Here the young Abbot at 25 years of age was able to define his conception of monastic life and set about putting it into practice. In looking at the discipline of other monasteries, Bernard firmly recalled the need for a

Giovanni da Milano, *The Virgin Mary appears to St Bernard,* detail of a polyptic with the lives of the Saints, Museo Civico, Prato

sober and measured life, at table as in clothing and monastic buildings, and recommended the support and care of the poor. In the meantime the community of Clairvaux became ever more numerous and its foundations multiplied.

In those same years before 1130 Bernard started a prolific correspondence with many people of both important and modest social status. To the many *Epistolae* of this period must be added numerous *Sermones*, as well as *Sententiae* and *Tractatus*. Bernard's great friendship with William, Abbot of Saint-Thierry, and with William of Champeaux, among the most important figures of the 12th century, also date to this period. As from 1130, Bernard began to concern himself with many serious matters of the Holy See and of the Church. For this reason he was obliged to leave his monastery ever more frequently and he sometimes also travelled outside France. He founded several women's monasteries and was the protagonist of a lively correspondence with Peter the Venerable, Abbot of Cluny. In his polemical writings he targeted in particular Abelard, a great thinker who had conceived of a new approach to theology, introducing above all the dialectic and philosophical method in the construction of theological thought. On another front Bernard combated the heresy of the Cathars, who despised matter and the human body and consequently despised the Creator. On the other hand, he felt it was his duty to defend the Jews, and condemned the ever more widespread outbursts of anti-Semitism. With regard to this aspect of his apostolic action, several decades later Rabbi Ephraim of Bonn addressed a vibrant tribute to Bernard. In the same period the holy Abbot wrote his most famous works such as the celebrated *Sermons on the Song of Songs [In Canticum Sermones]*. In the last years of his life – he

Filippino Lippi, *The Virgin Mary appears to St Bernard*, detail, Badia, Florence

SVBSTINE
ET ABSTINE

died in 1153 – Bernard was obliged to curtail his journeys but did not entirely stop travelling. He made the most of this time to review definitively the whole collection of his *Letters, Sermons* and *Treatises*. Worthy of mention is a quite unusual book that he completed in this same period, in 1145, when Bernardo Pignatelli, a pupil of his, was elected Pope with the name of Eugene III. On this occasion, Bernard as his spiritual father, dedicated to his spiritual son the text *De Consideratione* [Five Books on Consideration] which contains teachings on how to be a good Pope. In this book, which is still appropriate reading for the Popes of all times, Bernard did not only suggest how to be a good Pope, but also expressed a profound vision of the Mystery of the Church and of the Mystery of Christ which is ultimately resolved in contemplation of the mystery of the Triune God. "The search for this God who is not yet sufficiently sought must be continued", the holy Abbot wrote, "yet it may be easier to search for him and find him in prayer rather than in discussion. So let us end the book here, but not the search" (XIV, 32: *PL* 182, 808) and in journeying on towards God.

I would now like to reflect on only two of the main aspects of Bernard's rich doctrine: they concern Jesus Christ and Mary Most Holy, his Mother. His concern for the Christian's intimate and vital participation in God's love in Jesus Christ brings no new guidelines to the scientific status of theology. However, in a more decisive manner than ever, the Abbot of Clairvaux embodies the theologian, the contemplative and the mystic. Jesus alone Bernard insists in the face of the complex dialectical reasoning of his time Jesus alone is "honey in the mouth, song to the ear, jubilation in the heart (*mel in ore, in aure melos, in corde iubilum*)". The title *Doctor Mellifluus*, attributed to Bernard by tradition, stems precisely from this;

St Bernard and the devil, Florence Charterhouse

Simone dei Crocifissi, *St Bernard gives the rule*, Pinacoteca Nazionale, Bologna

indeed, his praise of Jesus Christ "flowed like honey". In the extenuating battles between Nominalists and Realists two philosophical currents of the time the Abbot of Clairvaux never tired of repeating that only one name counts, that of Jesus of Nazareth. "All food of the soul is dry", he professed, "unless it is moistened with this oil; insipid, unless it is seasoned with this salt. What you write has no savour for me unless I have read Jesus in it" (*In Canticum Sermones* XV, 6: *PL* 183, 847). For Bernard, in fact, true knowledge of God consisted in a personal, profound experience of Jesus Christ and of his love. And, dear brothers and sisters, this is true for every Christian: faith is first and foremost a personal, intimate encounter with Jesus, it is having an experience of his closeness, his friendship and his love. It is in this way that we learn to know him ever better, to love him and to follow him more and more. May this happen to each one of us!

In another famous *Sermon on the Sunday in the Octave of the Assumption*, the Holy Abbot described with passionate words Mary's intimate participation in the redeeming sacrifice of her Son. "O Blessed Mother", he exclaimed, "a sword has truly pierced your soul!... So deeply has the violence of pain pierced your soul, that we may rightly call you more than a martyr for in you participation in the passion of the Son by far surpasses in intensity the physical sufferings of martyrdom" (14: *PL* 183, 437-438). Bernard had no doubts: "*per Mariam ad Iesum*", through Mary we are led to Jesus. He testifies clearly to Mary's subordination to Jesus, in accordance with the foundation of traditional Mariology. Yet the text of the *Sermone* also documents the Virgin's privileged place in the economy of salvation, subsequent to the Mother's most particular participation (*compassio*) in the sacrifice of the Son. It is not for nothing that a century and a half after Bernard's death, Dante Alighieri, in the last canticle of the *Divine Comedy*, was to put on the lips of the *Doctor Mellifluus* the sublime prayer to Mary: "Virgin Mother, daughter of your own Son, / humble and exalted more than any creature, / fixed term of the eternal counsel" (*Paradise* XXXIII, vv. 1 ff).

These reflections, characteristic of a person in love with Jesus and Mary as was Bernard, are still a salutary stimulus not only to theologians but to all believers. Some claim to have solved the fundamental questions on God, on man and on the world with the power of reason alone. St Bernard, on the other hand, solidly founded on the Bible and on the Fathers of the Church, reminds us that without a profound faith in God, nourished by prayer and contemplation, by an intimate relationship with the Lord, our reflections on the divine mysteries risk becoming an empty intellectual exercise and losing their credibility. Theology refers us back to the "knowledge of the Saints", to their intuition of the mysteries of the living God and to their wisdom, a gift of the Holy Spirit, which become a reference point for theological thought. Together with Bernard of Clairvaux, we too must recognise that man seeks God better and finds him more easily "in prayer than in discussion". In the end, the truest figure of a theologian and of every evangeliser remains the Apostle John who laid his head on the Teacher's breast.

I would like to conclude these reflections on St Bernard with the invocations to Mary that we read in one of his beautiful homilies. "In danger, in distress, in uncertainty", he says, "think of Mary, call upon Mary. She never leaves your lips, she never departs from your heart; and so that you may obtain the help of her prayers, never forget the example of her life. If you follow her, you cannot falter; if you pray to her, you cannot despair; if you think of her, you cannot err. If she sustains you, you will not stumble; if she protects you, you have nothing to fear; if she guides you, you will never flag; if she is favourable to you, you will attain your goal..." (*Hom. II super "Missus est",* 17: *PL* 183, 70-71).

Monastic Theology and Scholastic Theology

Let us now reflect on an interesting page of history that concerns the flourishing of Latin theology in the 12th century which occurred through a series of providential coincidences. A relative peace prevailed in the countries of Western Europe at that time which guaranteed economic development and the consolidation of political structures in society, encouraging lively cultural activity also through its contacts with the East. The benefits of the vast action known as the "Gregorian reform" were already being felt within the Church. Vigorously promoted in the previous century, they had brought greater evangelical purity to the life of the ecclesial community, especially to the clergy, and had restored to the Church and to the Papacy authentic freedom of action. Furthermore, a wide-scale spiritual renewal supported by the vigorous development of consecrated life was spreading; new religious orders were coming into being and expanding, while those already in existence were experiencing a promising spiritual revival.

Justus of Gand and Pedro Berreguete, *St Thomas Aquinas*, Louvre, Paris

Theology also flourished anew, acquiring a greater awareness of its own nature: it refined its method; it tackled the new problems; advanced in the contemplation of God's mysteries; produced fundamental works; inspired important initiatives of culture, from art to literature; and prepared the masterpieces of the century to come, the century of Thomas Aquinas and Bonaventure of Bagnoregio. This intense theological activity took place in two milieus: the monasteries and the urban Schools, the *scholae*, some of which were the forerunners of universities, one of the characteristic "inventions" of the Christian Middle Ages. It is on the basis of these two milieus, monasteries and *scholae*, that it is possible to speak of the two different theological models: "monastic theology" and "scholastic theology". The representatives of monastic theology were monks, usually abbots, endowed with wisdom and evangelical zeal, dedicated essentially to inspiring and nourishing God's loving design. The representatives of Scholastic theology were cultured men, passionate about research; they were *magistri* anxious to show the reasonableness and soundness of the Mysteries of God and of man, believed with faith, of course, but also understood by reason. Their different finalities explain the differences in their method and in their way of doing theology.

In 12th-century monasteries the theological method mainly entailed the explanation of Sacred Scripture, the *sacra pagina* to borrow the words of the authors of that period; biblical theology in particular was practised. The monks, in other words, were devout listeners to and readers of the Sacred Scriptures and one of their chief occupations consisted in *lectio divina*, that is, the prayed reading of the Bible. For them the mere reading of the Sacred Text did not suffice to perceive its profound meaning, its inner unity and transcendent message.

It was therefore necessary to practise a biblical theology, in docility to the Holy Spirit. Thus, at the school of the Fathers, the Bible was interpreted allegorically in order to discover on every page of both the Old and New Testaments what it says about Christ and his work of salvation.

Last year, the Synod of Bishops on the "Word of God in the life and mission of the Church" reminded us of the importance of the spiritual approach to the Sacred Scriptures. It is useful for this purpose to take into account monastic theology, an uninterrupted biblical exegesis, as well as the works written by its exponents, precious ascetic commentaries on the Books of the Bible. Thus monastic theology incorporated the spiritual aspect into literary formation. It was aware, in other words that a purely theoretical and unversed interpretation is not enough: to enter into the heart of Sacred Scripture it must be read in the spirit in which it was written and created. Literary knowledge was necessary in order to understand the exact meaning of the words and to grasp the meaning of the text, refining the grammatical and philological sensibility. Thus *Jean Leclercq*, a Benedictine scholar in the past century, entitled the essay in which he presents the characteristics of monastic theology: *L'amour des lettres et le désir de Dieu* (Love of words and the desire for God). In fact, the desire to know and to love God which comes to meet us through his words to be received, meditated upon and put into practice, leads us to seek to deepen our knowledge of the biblical texts in all their dimensions. Then there is another attitude on which those who practise monastic theology insist: namely an intimate, prayerful disposition that must precede, accompany and complete the study of Sacred Scripture. Since, ultimately, monastic theology is listening to God's word, it is impossible not to purify the heart in order to receive it and, especially, it is impossible not to enkindle in it a longing to encounter the Lord. Theology thus becomes meditation, prayer, a song of praise and impels us to sincere conversion. On this path, many exponents of monastic theology attained the highest goals of mystic experience and extend an invitation to us too to nourish our lives with the word of God, for example, through listening more attentively to the Readings and the Gospel, especially during Sunday Mass. It is also important to set aside a certain period each day for meditation on the Bible, so that the word of God may be a light that illumines our daily pilgrimage on earth.

Scholastic theology, on the other hand as I was saying was practised at the *scholae* which came into being beside the great cathedrals of that time for the formation of the clergy, or around a teacher of theology and his disciples, to train professionals of culture in a period in which the appreciation of knowledge was constantly growing. Central to the method of the Scholastics was the *quaestio*, that is, the problem the reader faces in approaching the words of Scripture and of Tradition. In the face of the problem that these authoritative texts pose, questions arise and the debate between teacher and student comes into being. In this discussion, on the one hand the arguments of the authority appear and on the other those of reason, and the ensuing discussion seeks to come to a synthesis between authority and reason in order to reach a deeper understanding of the word of God. In this regard St Bonaventure said that theology is "*per additionem*" (cf. *Commentaria in quatuor libros sententiarum,* I, *proem.,* q. 1, *concl.*), that is, theology adds the dimension of reason to the word of God and thus creates a faith that is deeper, more personal, hence also more concrete in the

Victor Crivelli, *St Bonaventure,* Musée Jacquemart-André

OPVS VICTOR CRIVELLIV VENETII

person's life. In this regard various solutions were found and conclusions reached which began to build a system of theology. The organisation of the *quaestiones* led to the compilation of ever more extensive syntheses, that is, the different *quaestiones* were composed with the answers elicited, thereby creating a synthesis, the summae that were in reality extensive theological and dogmatic treatises born from the confrontation of human reason with the word of God. Scholastic theology aimed to present the unity and harmony of the Christian Revelation with a method, called, precisely "Scholastic" of the school which places trust in human reason. Grammar and philology are at the service of theological knowledge, but logic even more so, namely the discipline that studies the "functioning" of human reasoning, in such a way that the truth of a proposal appears obvious. Still today, in reading the Scholastic *summae* one is struck by the order, clarity and logical continuity of the arguments and by the depth of certain insights. With technical language a precise meaning is attributed to every word and, between believing and understanding, a reciprocal movement of clarification is established.

In echoing the invitation of the *First Letter of Peter*, Scholastic theology stimulates us to be ever ready to account for the hope that is in us (cf. 3: 15), hearing the questions as our own and thus also being capable of giving an answer. It reminds us that a natural friendship exists between faith and reason, founded in the order of Creation itself. In the *incipit* of the Encyclical *Fides et Ratio*, the Servant of God John Paul II wrote: "Faith and reason are like two wings on which the human spirit rises to the contemplation of truth". Faith is open to the effort of understanding by reason; reason, in turn, recognises that faith does not mortify her but on the contrary impels her towards vaster and loftier horizons. The eternal lesson of monastic theology fits in here. Faith and reason, in reciprocal dialogue, are vibrant with joy when they are both inspired by the search for intimate union with God. When love enlivens the prayerful dimension of theology, knowledge, acquired by reason, is broadened. Truth is sought with humility, received with wonder and gratitude: in a word, knowledge only grows if one loves truth. Love becomes intelligence and authentic theology wisdom of the heart, which directs and sustains the faith and life of believers. Let us therefore pray that the journey of knowledge and of the deepening of God's Mysteries may always be illumined by divine love.

Vergine madre fillia del tuo fillio
humile et alta piu che creatura
termine fisso deterno consillo
Tu se colei che lumana natura
nobilitasti sichel suo factore
no disdegno difarsi sua factura
Nel uentre tuo siraccese lamore
plo cui caldo neleterna pace
cosi e germinato questo fiore
Qui se anoi meridiana face
dicaritade et giuso intra mortali
se disperanza fontana uiuace
Donna se tanto grande et tanto uali
che qual uuol grã et adte nõ ricorre
sua disianza uuol uolar sanzali
La tua benignita nõ pur soccorre
achi dimanda ma molte fiate
liberamẽte aldimandar precorre
Inte misericordia inte pietate
inte magnificentia inte saduna
quantũque in creatura e dibontate
Or questi che dalinfima alachuna
delluniuerso infinqui auedute
leuite spiritali aduna aduna
Supplica adte pergratia diuirtute
tanto che possa colliochi leuarsi
piu alto uerso lultima salute
Et io che mai pmio ueder nõnarsi
piu chio fo plisuoi tucti miei ꝑeghi
tipriego et ꝑego che nõ sieno scarsi
Per che tu ogni nube lidisleghi
disua mortalita copriegli tuoi
sichel somo piacer li sidispieghi
Ancor tipriego regina che puoi
cio che tu uuoi cheli conserui sani
dopo tanto ueder liaffecti suoi
Uinca tua gratia imouimẽti humani
uedi beatrice con quãti beati
pli miei ꝑeghi tichiudon lemani

Two Theological Models in Comparison: Bernard and Abelard

The main features of 12th-century monastic theology and scholastic theology might be called respectively "theology of the heart" and "theology of reason". Among the exponents of both these theological currents a broad and at times heated discussion developed, symbolically represented by the controversy between St Bernard of Clairvaux and Abelard.

In order to understand this confrontation between the two great teachers it helps to remember that theology is the search for a rational understanding, as far as this is possible, of the mysteries of Christian Revelation, believed through faith: *fides quaerens intellectum* faith seeks understanding to borrow a traditional, concise and effective definition. Now, whereas St Bernard, a staunch representative of monastic theology, puts the accent on the first part of the definition, namely on *fides* – faith, Abelard, who was a scholastic, insists on the second part, that is, on the *intellectus*, on understanding through reason. For

St Bernard and Dante before the Virgin Mary, miniature Divine Comedy by Dante Alighieri, Ms Yates Thompson 36, fol. 189r, British Library, London

Bernard faith itself is endowed with a deep certitude based on the testimony of Scripture and on the teaching of the Church Fathers. Faith, moreover, is reinforced by the witness of the Saints and by the inspiration of the Holy Spirit in the individual believer's soul. In cases of doubt and ambiguity, faith is protected and illumined by the exercise of the Magisterium of the Church. So it was that Bernard had difficulty in reaching agreement with Abelard and, more in general, with those who submitted the truths of faith to the critical examination of the intellect; an examination which in his opinion entailed a serious danger, that is, intellectualism, the relativisation of truth, the questioning of the actual truths of faith. In this approach Bernard saw audacity taken to the point of unscrupulousness, a product of the pride of human intelligence that claims to "grasp" the mystery of God. In a letter he writes with regret: "Human ingenuity takes possession of everything, leaving nothing to faith. It confronts what is above and beyond it, scrutinises what is superior to it, bursts into the world of God, alters rather than illumines the mysteries of faith; it does not open what is closed and sealed but rather uproots it, and what it does not find viable in itself it considers as nothing and refuses to believe in it" (*Epistola* CLXXXVIII,1: *PL* 182, 1, 353).

Theology for Bernard had a single purpose: to encourage the intense and profound experience of God. Theology is therefore an aid to loving the Lord ever more and ever better, as the title of his Treatise on the *Duty to love God* says (*Liber de diligendo Deo*). On this journey there are various stages that Bernard describes in detail, which lead to the crowning experience when the believer's soul becomes inebriated in ineffable love. Already on earth the human soul can attain this mystical union with

Jan Foquet, *St Bernard teaching*, miniature from *Le Livre d'Heures d'Etienne* Chevalier, Ms. 71, fol. 40r, Musée Condé, Chantilly

the divine Word, a union that the *Doctor Mellifluus* describes as "spiritual nuptials". The divine Word visits the soul, eliminates the last traces of resistance, illuminates, inflames and transforms it. In this mystical union the soul enjoys great serenity and sweetness and sings a hymn of joy to its Bridegroom. As I mentioned in the Catechesis on the life and doctrine of St Bernard, theology for him could not but be nourished by contemplative prayer, in other words by the affective union of the heart and the mind with God.

On the other hand Abelard, who among other things was the very person who introduced the term "theology" in the sense in which we understand it today, puts himself in a different perspective. Born in Brittany, France, this famous teacher of the 12th century was endowed with a keen intelligence and his vocation was to study. He first concerned himself with philosophy and then applied the results he achieved in this discipline to theology which he taught in Paris, the most cultured city of the time, and later in the monasteries in which he lived. He was a brilliant orator: literally crowds of students attended his lectures. He had a religious spirit but a restless personality and his life was full of dramatic events: he contested his teachers and he had a son by Héloïse, a cultured and intelligent woman. He often argued with his theological colleagues and also underwent ecclesiastical condemnations although he died in full communion with the Church, submitting to her authority with a spirit of faith. Actually St Bernard contributed to condemning certain teachings of Abelard at the Provincial Synod of Sens in 1140 and went so far as to request Pope Innocent II's intervention. The Abbot of Clairvaux contested, as we have seen, the excessively intellectualistic method of Abelard who in his eyes reduced faith to mere opinion, detached from the revealed truth.

Bernard's fears were not unfounded and were, moreover, shared by other great thinkers of his time. Indeed, an excessive use of philosophy dangerously weakened Abelard's Trinitarian teaching, hence also his idea of God. In the moral field his teaching was not devoid of ambiguity: he insisted on considering the intention of the subject as the sole source for defining the goodness or evil of moral acts, thereby neglecting the objective significance and moral value of the actions: a dangerous subjectivism. This as we know is a very timely aspect for our epoch in which all too often culture seems to be marked by a growing tendency to ethical relativism; the self alone decides what is good for it, for oneself, at this moment. However, the great merits of Abelard, who had many disciples and made a crucial contribution to the development of scholastic theology destined to be expressed in a more mature and fruitful manner in the following century should not be forgotten. Nor should some of his insights be underestimated, such as, for example, his affirmation that non-Christian religious traditions already contain a preparation for the acceptance of Christ, the divine Word.

What can we learn today from the confrontation, frequently in very heated tones, between Bernard and Abelard and, in general, between monastic theology and scholastic theology? First of all I believe that it demonstrates the usefulness and need for healthy theological discussion within the Church, especially when the questions under discussion are not defined by the Magisterium, which nevertheless remains an ineluctable reference point. St Bernard, but also Abelard himself, always recognised her authority unhesitatingly. Furthermore, Abelard's condemnation on various occasions reminds us that in the theological field there must be a balance between what we may call the architectural principles given to us by Revelation, which

Abelard and Heloise, miniature from the manuscript of *The Poems of Charles, Duke of Orleans*, British Library, London

therefore always retain their priority importance, and the principles for interpretation suggested by philosophy, that is, by reason, which have an important but exclusively practical role. When this balance between the architecture and the instruments for interpretation is lacking, theological reflection risks being distorted by errors and it is then the task of the Magisterium to exercise that necessary service to the truth which belongs to it. It must be emphasised in addition that among the reasons that induced Bernard to "take sides" against Abelard and to call for the intervention of the Magisterium, was also his concern to safeguard simple and humble believers, who must be defended when they risk becoming confused or misled by excessively personal opinions or by anti-conformist theological argumentation that might endanger their faith.

Lastly, I would like to recall that the theological confrontation between Bernard and Abelard ended with their complete reconciliation, thanks to the mediation of a common friend, Peter the Venerable, the Abbot of Cluny of whom we have already spoken. Abelard showed humility in recognising his errors, Bernard used great benevolence. They both upheld the most important value in a theological controversy: to preserve the Church's faith and to make the truth in charity triumph. Today too may this be the attitude with which we confront one another in the Church, having as our goal the constant quest for truth.

The Cluniac Reform

The Order of Cluny at the beginning of the 12th century, at the height of its expansion, had almost 1,200 monasteries: a truly impressive figure! A monastery was founded at Cluny in 910, precisely 1,100 years ago, and subsequent to the donation of William the Pious, Duke of Aquitaine, was placed under the guidance of Abbot Berno. At that time Western monasticism, which had flourished several centuries earlier with St Benedict, was experiencing a severe decline for various reasons: unstable political and social conditions due to the continuous invasions and sacking by peoples who were not integrated into the fabric of Europe, widespread poverty and, especially, the dependence of abbeys on the local nobles who controlled all that belonged to the territories under their jurisdiction. In this context, Cluny was the heart and soul of a profound renewal of monastic life that led it back to its original inspiration.

At Cluny the Rule of St Benedict was restored with several adaptations which had already been introduced by other reformers. The main objective was to guarantee the central role

Cluny Abbey internal view, drawing, Bibliothèque nationale de France, Paris that the Liturgy must have in Christian life. The Cluniac monks devoted themselves with love and great care to the celebration of the Liturgical Hours, to the singing of the Psalms, to processions as devout as they were solemn, and above all, to the celebration of Holy Mass. They promoted sacred music, they wanted architecture and art to contribute to the beauty and solemnity of the rites; they enriched the liturgical calendar with special celebrations such as, for example, at the beginning of November, the Commemoration of All Souls, which we too have just celebrated; and they intensified the devotion to the Virgin Mary. Great importance was given to the Liturgy because the monks of Cluny were convinced that it was participation in the liturgy of Heaven. And the monks felt responsible for interceding at the altar of God for the living and the dead, given large numbers of the faithful were insistently asking them to be remembered in prayer. Moreover, it was with this same aim that William the Pious had desired the foundation of the Abbey of Cluny. In the ancient document that testifies to the foundation we read: "With this gift I establish that a monastery of regulars be built at Cluny in honour of the Holy Apostles Peter and Paul, where monks who live according to the Rule of St Benedict shall gather... so that a venerable sanctuary of prayer with vows and supplications may be visited there, and the heavenly life be sought after and yearned for with every desire and with deep ardour, and that assiduous prayers, invocations and supplications be addressed to the Lord". To preserve and foster this atmosphere of prayer, the Cluniac Rule emphasised the importance of silence, to which discipline the monks willingly submitted, convinced that the purity of the virtues to which they aspired demanded deep and constant recollection. It is not surprising that before long the Monastery of Cluny gained a reputation for holiness and that many other monastic communities decided to follow its discipline. Numerous princes and Popes asked the abbots of Cluny to extend their reform so that in a short time a dense network of monasteries developed that were linked to Cluny, either by true and proper juridical bonds or by a sort of charismatic affiliation. Thus a spiritual Europe gradually took shape in the various regions of France and in Italy, Spain, Germany and Hungary.

Cluny's success was assured primarily not only by the lofty spirituality cultivated there but also by several other conditions that ensured its development. In comparison with what had happened until then, the Monastery of Cluny and the communities dependent upon it were recognised as exempt from the jurisdiction of the local Bishops and were directly subject to that of the Roman Pontiff. This meant that Cluny had a special bond with the See of Peter and, precisely because of the protection and encouragement of the Pontiffs, the ideals of purity and fidelity proposed by the Cluniac Reform spread rapidly. Furthermore, the abbots were elected without any interference from the civil authorities, unlike what happened in other places. Truly worthy people succeeded one another at the helm of Cluny and of the numerous monastic communities dependent upon it: Abbot Odo of Cluny and other great figures such as Eymard, Majolus, Odilo and especially Hugh the Great, who served for long periods, thereby assuring stability and the spread of the reform embarked upon. As well as Odo, Majolus, Odilo and Hugh are venerated as Saints.

Not only did the Cluniac Reform have positive effects in the purification and reawakening of monastic life but also in the

Double Page spread: *Pope Urban II confirming the privileges of Cluny Abbey,* miniature from the *Chronicles of Cluny Abbey,* Ms lat. 17716, fol. 91r, Bibliothèque nationale de France, Paris

pmus cancellis sacrarunt alta
ria. Tunc papa int[er]ea sacrando mis
sasq; agendo. p[ost] alia salutis hor
tam[en]ta. cora[m] ep[iscop]is & cardinalibus
multor[um]q; p[er]sonis. Huiuscemodi
[illegible] habuit ad p[o]p[u]l[u]m.

s. romanu scilicet pontificio
ior numero uel ordini diuina
e dignatio licet indignum as
ciauit: me olim monachum
iorem q; monasterii huius. sub
mno ac uenerabili hugone

life of the universal Church. In fact, the aspiration to evangelical perfection was an incentive to fight two great abuses that afflicted the Church in that period: simony, that is the acquisition of pastoral offices for money, and immorality among the secular clergy. The abbots of Cluny with their spiritual authority, the Cluniac monks who became Bishops and some of them even Popes, took the lead in this impressive action of spiritual renewal. And it yielded abundant fruit: celibacy was once again esteemed and practised by priests and more transparent procedures were introduced in the designation of ecclesiastical offices.

Also significant were the benefits that monasteries inspired by the Cluniac Reform contributed to society. At a time when Church institutions alone provided for the poor, charity was practised with dedication. In all the houses, the almoner was bound to offer hospitality to needy wayfarers and pilgrims, travelling priests and religious and especially the poor, who came asking for food and a roof over their heads for a few days. Equally important were two other institutions promoted by Cluny that were characteristic of medieval civilisation: the "Truce of God" and the "Peace of God". In an epoch heavily marked by violence and the spirit of revenge, with the "Truces of God" long periods of non-belligerence were guaranteed, especially on the occasion of specific religious feasts and certain days of the week. With "the Peace of God", on pain of a canonical reprimand, respect was requested for defenceless people and for sacred places.

In this way, the conscience of the peoples of Europe matured during that long process of gestation, which was to lead to their ever clearer recognition of the two fundamental elements for the construction of society, namely, the value of the human person and the primary good of peace. Furthermore, as happened for other monastic foundations, the Cluniac monasteries had likewise at their disposal extensive properties which, diligently put to good use, helped to develop the economy. Alongside the manual work there was no lack of the typical cultural activities of medieval monasticism such as schools for children, the foundation of libraries and *scriptoria* for the transcription of books.

In this way, 1,000 years ago when the development of the European identity had gathered momentum, the experience of Cluny, which had spread across vast regions of the European continent, made its important and precious contribution. It recalled the primacy of spiritual benefits; it kept alive the aspiration to the things of God; it inspired and encouraged initiatives and institutions for the promotion of human values; it taught a spirit of peace. Let us pray that all those who have at heart an authentic humanism and the future of Europe may be able to rediscover, appreciate and defend the rich cultural and religious heritage of these centuries.

The Cathedral from Romanesque to Gothic Architecture: The Theological Background

In the preceding chapters I have presented several aspects of medieval theology. The Christian faith, however, deeply rooted in the men and women of those centuries, did not only give rise to masterpieces of theological literature, thought and faith. It also inspired one of the loftiest expressions of universal civilisation: the cathedral, the true glory of the Christian Middle Ages. Indeed, for about three centuries, from the beginning of the 11th century Europe experienced extraordinary artistic creativity and fervour. An ancient chronicler described the enthusiasm and the hard-working spirit of those times in these words: "It happens that throughout the world, but especially in Italy and in Gaul, people began rebuilding churches although many had no need of such restoration because they were still in good condition. "It was like a competition between one people and another; one might have believed that the world, shaking off its rags and tatters, wanted to be reclad throughout in the white mantle of new churches. In short, all these cathedral churches, a large number of monastic churches and even village oratories, were restored by the faithful at that time" (Rodolphus Glaber, *Historiarum, libri quinque,* 3, 4).

Various factors contributed to this rebirth of religious architecture. First of all more favourable historical conditions,

Cathedral of St Peter, Trier

such as greater political stability, accompanied by a constant increase in the population and the gradual development of the cities, trade and wealth. Furthermore, architects found increasingly complicated technical solutions to increase the size of buildings, at the same time guaranteeing them both soundness and majesty. It was mainly thanks to the enthusiasm and spiritual zeal of monasticism, at the height of its expansion, that abbey churches were built in which the Liturgy might be celebrated with dignity and solemnity. They became the destination of continuous pilgrimages where the faithful, attracted by the veneration of saints' relics, could pause in prayer. So it was that the Romanesque churches and cathedrals came into being. They were characterised by the longitudinal development, in length, of the aisles, in order to accommodate numerous faithful. They were very solid churches with thick walls, stone vaults and simple, spare lines. An innovation was the introduction of sculptures. Because Romanesque churches were places for monastic prayer and for the worship of the faithful, rather than being concerned with technical perfection, the sculptors turned their attention in particular to the educational dimension. Since it was necessary to inspire in souls strong impressions, sentiments that could persuade them to shun vice and evil and to practise virtue and goodness, the recurrent theme was the portrayal of Christ as Universal Judge surrounded by figures of the Apocalypse. It was usually the portals of the Romanesque churches which displayed these figures, to emphasise that Christ is the Door that leads to Heaven. On crossing the threshold of the sacred building, the faithful entered a space and time different from that of their ordinary life. Within the church, believers in a sovereign, just and merciful Christ in the artists' intention could enjoy in anticipation

Last Judgment, West door, Cathedral of St-Lazare, Autun

eternal beatitude in the celebration of the liturgy and of devotional acts carried out in the sacred building.

In the 12th and 13th centuries another kind of architecture for sacred buildings spread from the north of France: the Gothic. It had two new characteristics in comparison with the Romanesque, a soaring upward movement and luminosity. Gothic cathedrals show a synthesis of faith and art harmoniously expressed in the fascinating universal language of beauty which still elicits wonder today. By the introduction of vaults with pointed arches supported by robust pillars, it was possible to increase their height considerably. The upward thrust was intended as an invitation to prayer and at the same time was itself a prayer. Thus the Gothic cathedral intended to express in its architectural lines the soul's longing for God. In addition, by employing the new technical solutions, it was possible to make openings in the outer walls and to embellish them with stained-glass windows. In other words the windows became great luminous images, very suitable for instructing the people in faith. In them scene by scene the life of a saint, a parable or some other biblical event were recounted. A cascade of light poured through the stained-glass upon the faithful to tell them the story of salvation and to involve them in this story.

Another merit of Gothic cathedrals is that the whole Christian and civil community participated in their building and decoration in harmonious and complementary ways. The lowly and the powerful, the illiterate and the learned; all participated because in this common house all believers were instructed in the faith. Gothic sculpture in fact has made cathedrals into "stone Bibles", depicting Gospel episodes and illustrating the content of the liturgical year, from the Nativity to the glorification of the Lord.

Abbey of Saint Denis, Paris

In those centuries too, the perception of the Lord's humanity became ever more widespread and the sufferings of his Passion were represented realistically: the suffering Christ (*Christus patiens*) an image beloved by all and apt to inspire devotion and repentance for sins. Nor were Old Testament figures lacking; thus to the faithful who went to the cathedral their histories became familiar as part of the one common history of salvation. With faces full of beauty, gentleness and intelligence, Gothic sculpture of the 13th century reveals a happy and serene religious sense, glad to show a heartfelt filial devotion to the Mother of God, sometimes seen as a young woman, smiling and motherly, but mainly portrayed as the Queen of Heaven and earth, powerful and merciful. The faithful who thronged the Gothic cathedrals also liked to find there, expressed in works of art, saints, models of Christian life and intercessors with God. And there was no shortage of the "secular" scenes of life, thus, here and there, there are depictions of work in the fields, of the sciences and arts. All was oriented and offered to God in the place in which the Liturgy was celebrated. We may understand better the meaning attributed to a Gothic cathedral by reflecting on the text of the inscription engraved on the central portal of Saint-Denis in Paris: "Passerby, who is stirred to praise the beauty of these doors, do not let yourself be dazzled by the gold or by the magnificence, but rather by the painstaking work. Here a famous work shines out, but may Heaven deign that this famous work that shines make spirits resplendent so that, with the luminous truth, they may walk toward the true light, where Christ is the true door".

I would like to emphasise two elements of Romanesque and Gothic art that are also helpful to us. The first: the masterpieces of art created in Europe in past centuries are incomprehensible unless one takes into account the religious spirit that inspired them. Marc Chagall, an artist who has always witnessed to the encounter between aesthetics and faith, wrote that "For centuries painters dipped their brushes into that colourful alphabet which was the Bible". When faith, celebrated in the Liturgy in a special way, encounters art, it creates a profound harmony because each can and wishes to speak of God, making the Invisible visible. I would like to share this encounter with artists on 21 November, renewing to them the proposal of friendship between Christian spirituality and art that my venerable Predecessors hoped for, especially the Servants of God Paul VI and John Paul II. The second element: the strength of the Romanesque style and the splendour of the Gothic cathedrals remind us that the *via pulchritudinis*, the way of beauty, is a privileged and fascinating path on which to approach the Mystery of God. What is the beauty that writers, poets, musicians, and artists contemplate and express in their language other than the reflection of the splendour of the eternal Word made flesh? Then St Augustine says: "Question the beauty of the earth, question the beauty of the sea, question the beauty of the air, amply spread around everywhere, question the beauty of the sky, question the serried ranks of the stars, question the sun making the day glorious with its bright beams, question the moon tempering the darkness of the following night with its shining rays, question the animals that move in the waters, that amble about on dry land, that fly in the air; their souls hidden, their bodies evident; the visible bodies needing to be controlled, the invisible souls controlling them. Question all these things. They all answer you, 'Here we are, look; we're beautiful!' Their beauty is their confession. Who made these beautiful changeable things, if not one who is beautiful and unchangeable?" (*Sermo CCXLI*, 2: *PL* 38, 1134).

May the Lord help us to rediscover the way of beauty as one of the itineraries, perhaps the most attractive and fascinating, on which to succeed in encountering and loving God.

Hugh and Richard of Saint-Victor

Hugh and Richard of Saint-Victor were among those philosophers and theologians known as "Victorines" because they lived and taught at the Abbey of Saint-Victor in Paris, founded at the beginning of the 12th century by William of Champeaux. William himself was a well-known teacher who succeeded in giving his abbey a solid cultural identity. Indeed, a school for the formation of the monks, also open to external students, was founded at Saint-Victor, where a felicitous synthesis was achieved between the two theological models of which I have spoken. These are monastic theology, primarily oriented to contemplation of the mysteries of the faith in Scripture; and scholastic theology, which aimed to use reason to scrutinise these mysteries with innovative methods in order to create a theological system.

We have little information about the life of Hugh of Saint-Victor. The date and place of his birth are uncertain; he may have been born in Saxony or in Flanders. It is known that

Hugh of Saint Victor teaching a group of monks, miniature, Ms Laud. Misc. 409, fol. 3v, Bodleian Library, Oxford

having arrived in Paris the European cultural capital at that time he spent the rest of his days at the Abbey of Saint-Victor, where he was first a disciple and subsequently a teacher. Even before his death in 1141, he earned great fame and esteem, to the point that he was called a "second St Augustine". Like Augustine, in fact, he meditated deeply on the relationship between faith and reason, between the secular sciences and theology. According to Hugh of Saint-Victor, in addition to being useful for understanding the Scriptures, all the branches of knowledge have intrinsic value and must be cultivated in order to broaden human knowledge, as well as to answer the human longing to know the truth. This healthy intellectual curiosity led him to counsel students always to give free reign to their desire to learn. In his treatise on the methodology of knowledge and pedagogy, entitled significantly *Didascalicon (On Teaching)* his recommendation was: "Learn willingly what you do not know from everyone. The person who has sought to learn something from everyone will be wiser than them all. The person who receives something from everyone ends by becoming the richest of all" (*Eruditiones Didascalicae,* 3, 14; *PL* 176, 774).

The knowledge with which the philosophers and theologians known as *Victorines* were concerned in particular was theology, which requires first and foremost the loving study of Sacred Scripture. In fact, in order to know God one cannot but begin with what God himself has chosen to reveal of himself in the Scriptures. In this regard Hugh of Saint-Victor is a typical representative of monastic theology, based entirely on biblical exegesis. To interpret Scripture he suggests the traditional patristic and medieval structure, namely, the literal and historical sense first of all, then the allegorical and anagogical and, lastly, the moral. These are four dimensions of the meaning of Scripture that are being rediscovered even today. For this reason one sees that in the text and in the proposed narrative a more profound meaning is concealed: the thread of faith that leads us heavenwards and guides us on this earth, teaching us how to live. Yet, while respecting these four dimensions of the meaning of Scripture, in an original way in comparison with his contemporaries, Hugh of Saint-Victor insists and this is something new on the importance of the historical and literal meaning. In other words before discovering the symbolic value, the deeper dimensions of the biblical text, it is necessary to know and to examine the meaning of the event as it is told in Scripture. Otherwise, he warns, using an effective comparison, one risks being like grammarians who do not know the elementary rules. To those who know the meaning of history as described in the Bible, human events appear marked by divine Providence, in accordance with a clearly ordained plan. Thus, for Hugh of Saint-Victor, history is neither the outcome of a blind destiny nor as meaningless as it might seem. On the contrary, the Holy Spirit is at work in human history and inspires the marvellous dialogue of human beings with God, their friend. This theological view of history highlights the astonishing and salvific intervention of God who truly enters and acts in history. It is almost as if he takes part in our history, while ever preserving and respecting the human being's freedom and responsibility.

Our author considered that the study of Sacred Scripture and its historical and literal meaning makes possible true and proper theology, that is, the systematic illustration of truths, knowledge of their structure, the illustration of the dogmas of the faith. He presents these in a solid synthesis in his Treatise *De Sacramentis Christianae Fidei* (*The Sacraments of the Christian Faith*). Among other things, he provides a definition of "sacrament" which, further perfected by other theologians, contains ideas that are still very interesting today. "The sacrament is a corporeal or material element proposed in an external and tangible way", he writes, "which by its likeness *makes present* an invisible and spiritual grace; it *signifies* it, because it was instituted to this end, and *contains* it, because it is capable of sanctifying" (9, 2: *PL* 176, 317). On the one hand is the visibility in the symbol, the "corporeity" of the gift of God. On the other hand, however, in him is concealed the divine grace that comes from the history of Jesus Christ, who himself created the fundamental symbols. Therefore, there are three elements that contribute to the definition of a sacrament, according to Hugh of Saint-Victor: the institution by Christ; the communication of grace; and the analogy between the visible or material element and the invisible element: the divine gifts. This vision is very close to our contemporary understanding, because the sacraments are presented with a language interwoven with symbols and images capable of speaking directly to the human heart. Today too it is important that liturgical animators, and priests in particular, with pastoral wisdom, give due weight to the signs proper to sacramental rites to this visibility and tangibility of Grace. They should pay special attention to catechesis, to ensure that all the faithful experience every celebration of the sacraments with devotion, intensity and spiritual joy.

Richard, who came from Scotland, was Hugh of Saint-Victor's worthy disciple. He was prior of the Abbey of Saint-Victor from 1162 to 1173, the year of his death. Richard too, of course, assigned a fundamental role to the study of the Bible but, unlike his master, gave priority to the allegorical sense, the symbolic meaning of Scripture. This is what he uses, for

The Levels of the Temple in Jerusalem, from the Commentary on the Book of Ezekiel by Richard of Saint-Victor, Harley Ms 461, fol. 26r, British Library, London

riore parte implem⁹. Erat autē ut supius dictum ē xl. v. cubitꝰ emissior in exteriori latere. & secundū hoc tota altitudo ab exteriori parte uidetur in. xc. cubitꝰ insurgere. Videtur uero ab exteriori parte duo cenacula. unū autem ab exteriori parte habe. & de tercio & infimo thalamo dictum esse. Et mensus ē portam a tecto thalami usq; ad tectum e i u s.

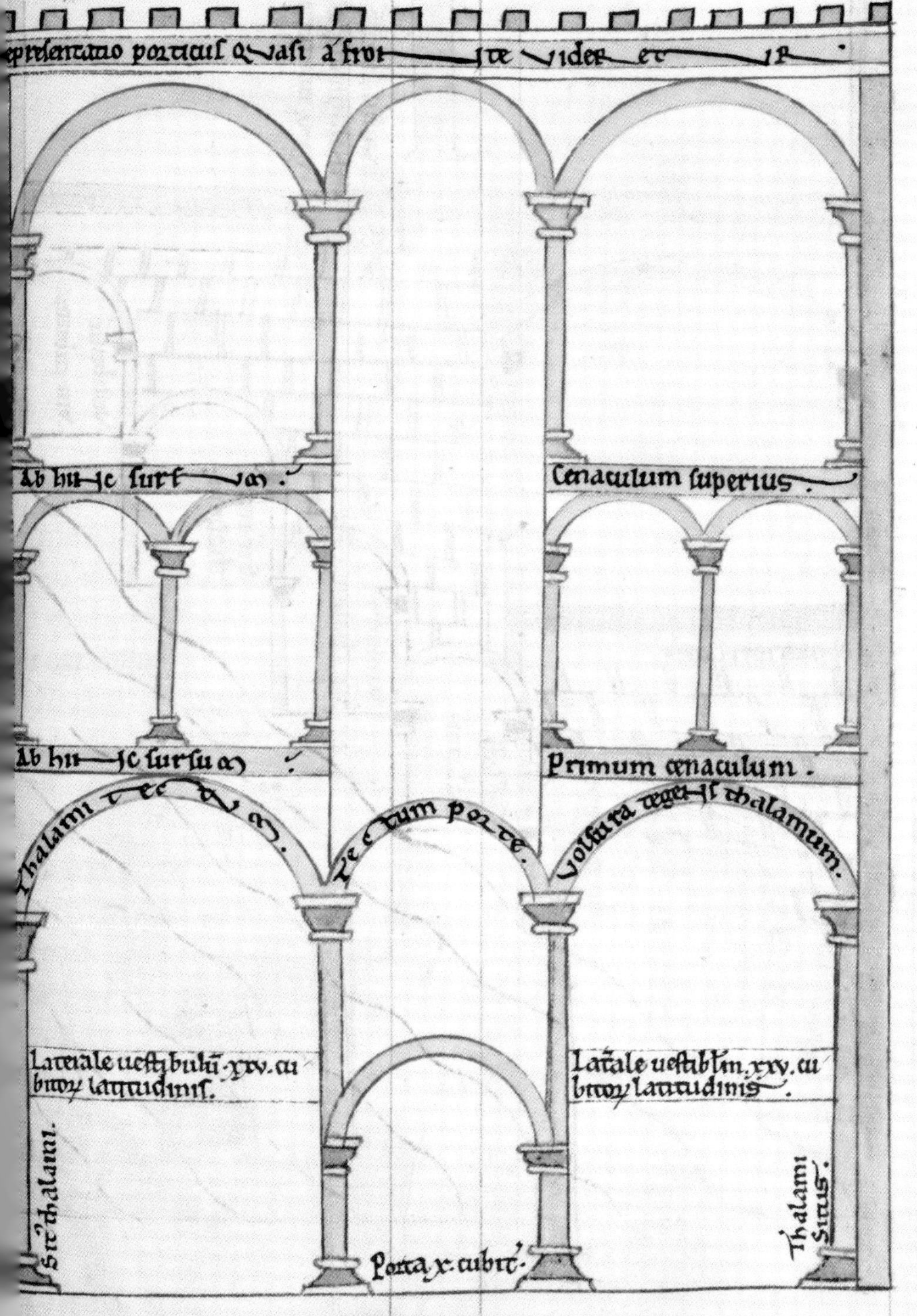

example, in his interpretation of the Old Testament figure of Benjamin, the son of Jacob, as a model of contemplation and the epitome of the spiritual life. Richard addresses this topic in two texts, *Benjamin Minor* and *Benjamin Maior*. In these he proposes to the faithful a spiritual journey which is primarily an invitation to exercise the various virtues, learning to discipline and to control with reason the sentiments and the inner affective and emotional impulses. Only when the human being has attained balance and human maturity in this area is he or she ready to approach contemplation, which Richard defines as "a profound and pure gaze of the soul, fixed on the marvels of wisdom, combined with an ecstatic sense of wonder and admiration" (*Benjamin Maior* 1,4: *PL* 196, 67).

Contemplation is therefore the destination, the result of an arduous journey that involves dialogue between faith and reason, that is once again a theological discourse. Theology stems from truths that are the subject of faith but seeks to deepen knowledge of them by the use of reason, taking into account the gift of faith. This application of reason to the comprehension of faith is presented convincingly in Richard's masterpiece, one of the great books of history, the *De Trinitate* (*The Trinity*). In the six volumes of which it is composed he reflects perspicaciously on the Mystery of the Triune God. According to our author, since God is love the one divine substance includes communication, oblation and love between the two Persons, the Father and the Son, who are placed in a reciprocal, eternal exchange of love. However the perfection of happiness and goodness admits of no exclusivism or closure. On the contrary, it requires the eternal presence of a third Person, the Holy Spirit. Trinitarian love is participatory, harmonious and includes a superabundance of delight, enjoyment and ceaseless joy. Richard, in other words, supposes that God is love, analyzes the essence of love of what the reality love entails and thereby arrives at the Trinity of the Persons, which really is the logical expression of the fact that God is love.

Yet Richard is aware that love, although it reveals to us the essence of God, although it makes us "understand" the Mystery of the Trinity, is nevertheless always an analogy that serves to speak of a Mystery that surpasses the human mind. Being the poet and mystic that he is, Richard also has recourse to other images. For example, he compares divinity to a river, to a loving wave which originates in the Father and ebbs and flows in the Son, to be subsequently spread with joy through the Holy Spirit.

Authors such as Hugh and Richard of Saint-Victor raise our minds to contemplation of the divine realities. At the same time, the immense joy we feel at the thought, admiration and praise of the Blessed Trinity supports and sustains the practical commitment to be inspired by this perfect model of communion in love in order to build our daily human relationships. The Trinity is truly perfect communion! How the world would change if relations were always lived in families, in parishes and in every other community by following the example of the three divine Persons in whom each lives not only *with* the other, but *for* the other and *in* the other! A few months ago at the Angelus I recalled: "Love alone makes us happy because we live in a relationship, and we live to love and to be loved" (*Angelus,* Trinity Sunday, 7 June 2009). It is love that works this ceaseless miracle. As in the life of the Blessed Trinity, plurality is recomposed in unity, where all is kindness and joy. With St Augustine, held in great honour by the *Victorines*, we too may exclaim: "*Vides Trinitatem, si caritatem vides* – you contemplate the Trinity, if you see charity" (*De Trinitate* VIII, 8, 12).

Cy commence le premier livre de la vie de monseigneur sainct bernard

Saint bernard fu nez en bourgoingne en ung chasteaulx de son ... qui est appellé fo...

William of Saint-Thierry

William was born in Liège between 1075 and 1080. He came from a noble family, was endowed with a keen intelligence and an innate love of study. He attended famous schools of the time, such as those in his native city and in Rheims, France. He also came into personal contact with Abelard, the teacher who applied philosophy to theology in such an original way as to give rise to great perplexity and opposition. William also expressed his own reservations, pressing his friend Bernard to take a stance concerning Abelard. Responding to God's mysterious and irresistible call which is the vocation to the consecrated life, William entered the Benedictine Monastery of Saint-Nicasius in Rheims in 1113. A few years later he became abbot of the Monastery of Saint-Thierry in the Diocese of Rheims. In that period there was a widespread need for the purification and renewal of monastic life to make it authentically evangelical. William worked on doing this in his own monastery and in general in the Benedictine Order. However, he met with great resistence to his attempts at reform and thus, although his friend Bernard

William of Saint-Thierry, Life and miracles of St Bernard,
Ms fr. 917, fol. 15r, Bibliothèque nationale de France, Paris

advised him against it, in 1135 he left the Benedictine abbey and exchanged his black habit for a white one in order to join the Cistercians of Signy. From that time, until his death in 1148, he devoted himself to prayerful contemplation of God's mysteries, ever the subject of his deepest desires, and to the composition of spiritual literature, important writings in the history of monastic theology.

One of his first works is entitled *De Natura et dignitate amoris* (*The nature and dignity of love*). In it William expressed one of his basic ideas that is also valid for us. The principal energy that moves the human soul, he said, is love. Human nature, in its deepest essence, consists in loving. Ultimately, a single task is entrusted to every human being: to learn to like and to love, sincerely, authentically and freely. However, it is only from God's teaching that this task is learned and that the human being may reach the end for which he was created. Indeed, William wrote: "The art of arts is the art of love.... Love is inspired by the Creator of nature. Love is a force of the soul that leads it as by a natural weight to its own place and end" (*De Natura et dignitate amoris* 1 *PL* 184, 379). Learning to love is a long and demanding process that is structured by William in four stages, corresponding to the ages of the human being: childhood, youth, maturity and old-age. On this journey the person must impose upon himself an effective ascesis, firm self-control to eliminate every irregular affection, every capitulation to selfishness, and to unify his own life in God, the source, goal and force of love, until he reaches the summit of spiritual life which William calls "wisdom". At the end of this ascetic process, the person feels deep serenity and sweetness. All the human being's faculties – intelligence, will, affection – rest in God, known and loved in Christ.

In other works too, William speaks of this radical vocation to love for God which is the secret of a successful and happy life and which he describes as a ceaseless, growing desire, inspired by God himself in the human heart. In a meditation he says "that the object of this love is Love" with a capital "L", namely God. It is he who pours himself out into the hearts of those who love him and prepares them to receive him. "God gives himself until the person is sated and in such a way that the desire is never lacking. This impetus of love is the fulfilment of the human being" (*De Contemplando Deo* 6, *passim,* SC 61 bis, pp. 79-83). The considerable importance that William gives to the emotional dimension is striking. Basically, dear friends, our hearts are made of flesh and blood, and when we love God, who is Love itself, how can we fail to express in this relationship with the Lord our most human feelings, such as tenderness, sensitivity and delicacy? In becoming Man, the Lord himself wanted to love us with a heart of flesh!

Moreover, according to William, love has another important quality: it illuminates the mind and enables one to know God better and more profoundly and, in God, people and events. The knowledge that proceeds from the senses and the intelligence reduces but does not eliminate the distance between the subject and the object, between the "I" and the "you". Love, on the other hand, gives rise to attraction and communion, to the point that transformation and assimilation take place between the subject who loves and the beloved object. This reciprocity of affection and liking subsequently permits a far deeper knowledge than that which is brought by reason alone. A famous saying of William expresses it: "*Amor ipse intellectus est* – love in itself is already the beginning of knowledge". Let us ask ourselves: is not our life just like this? Is it not perhaps true that we only truly know *who* and *what* we love? Without a certain fondness one knows no one and nothing! And this applies first of all to the knowledge of God and his mysteries that exceed our mental capacity to understand: God is known if he is loved!

A synthesis of William of Saint-Thierry's thought is contained in a long letter addressed to the Carthusians of Mont-Dieu, whom he visited and wished to encourage and console. Already in 1690, the learned Benedictine Jean Mabillon, gave this letter a meaningful title: *Epistola Aurea* (*Golden Epistle*). In fact, the teachings on spiritual life that it contains are invaluable for all those who wish to increase in communion with God and in holiness. In this treatise, William proposes an itinerary in three stages. It is necessary, he says, to move on from the "animal" being to the "rational" one, in order to attain to the "spiritual". What does our author mean by these three terms? To start with, a person accepts the vision of life inspired by faith with an act of obedience and trust. Then, with a process of interiorisation, in which the reason and the will play an important role, faith in Christ is received with profound conviction and one feels a harmonious correspondence between what is believed and what is hoped, and the most secret aspirations of the soul, our reason, our affections. One therefore arrives at the perfection of spiritual life when the realities of faith are a source of deep joy and real and satisfying communion with God. One lives only in love and for love. William based this process on a solid vision of the human being inspired by the ancient Greek Fathers, especially Origen who, with bold language, taught that the human being's vocation was to become like God who created him in his image and likeness. The image of God present in man impels him toward likeness, that is, toward an ever fuller identity between his own will and the divine will. One does not attain this perfection, which William calls "unity of spirit", by one's own efforts, even if they are sincere and generous, because something else is necessary. This perfection is reached through the action of the Holy Spirit who takes up his abode in the soul and purifies, absorbs and transforms into charity every impulse and desire of love that is present in the human being. "Then there is a further likeness to God", we read in the *Epistola Aurea*, "which is no longer called likeness but unity of spirit, when the person becomes one with God, one in spirit, not only because of the unity of an identical desire but through being unable to desire anything else. In this way the human being deserves to become not God but what God is: man becomes through grace what God is by nature" (*Epistola Aurea* 262-263, *SC* 223, pp. 353-355).

This author, whom we might describe as the "Singer of Charity, of Love", teaches us to make the basic decision in our lives which gives meaning and value to all our other decisions: to love God and, through love of him, to love our neighbour; only in this manner shall we be able to find true joy, an anticipation of eternal beatitude. Let us therefore learn from the Saints in order to learn to love authentically and totally, to set our being on this journey. Together with a young Saint, a Doctor of the Church, Thérèse of the Child Jesus, let us tell the Lord that we too want to live of love. And I conclude with a prayer precisely by this Saint: "You know I love you, Jesus Christ, my Own! Your Spirit's fire of love enkindles me. By loving you, I draw the Father here, down to my heart, to stay with me always. Blessed Trinity! You are my prisoner dear, of love, today.... To live of love, 'tis without stint to give. And never count the cost, nor ask reward.... O Heart Divine, o'erflowing with tenderness, How swift I run, who all to You has given! Naught but your love I need, my life to bless" [To live of love].

HIC . APERIT . TY
PICOSA . NOVE . SIGNACLA . LEGIS : QVĀ . STATVIT . SVB CARNE
NOVI . P̄SENTIA . REGIS
ROD PT . ABB̄ .

Rupert of Deutz

Rupert of Deutz, another 12th-century Benedictine monk, came from a city near Cologne, home to a famous monastery. Rupert himself speaks of his own life in one of his most important works entitled *The Glory and Honour of the Son of Man* [*De gloria et honore filii hominis super Matthaeum*], which is a commentary on part of the Gospel according to Matthew. While still a boy he was received at the Benedictine Monastery of St Laurence at Lièges as an "oblate", in accordance with the custom at that time of entrusting one of the sons to the monks for his education, intending to make him a gift to God. Rupert always loved monastic life. He quickly learned Latin in order to study the Bible and to enjoy the liturgical celebrations. He distinguished himself for his moral rectitude, straight as a die, and his strong attachment to the See of St Peter.

Rupert's time was marked by disputes between the Papacy and the Empire, because of the so-called "Investiture Controversy" with which as I have mentioned the Papacy wished to prevent the appointment of Bishops and the exercise of their jurisdiction from depending on the civil authorities

Rupert of Deutz, illustration from *De Officiis divines* by Rupert of Deutz, Cod. Lat. 14 355, fol. 1v, Staatsbibliothek, Munich

who were certainly not guided by pastoral reasons but for the most part by political and financial considerations. Bishop Otbert of Lièges resisted the Pope's directives and exiled Berengarius, Abbot of the Monastery of St Laurence, because of his fidelity to the Pontiff. It was in this monastery that Rupert lived. He did not hesitate to follow his Abbot into exile and only when Bishop Otbert returned to communion with the Pope did he return to Liège and agree to become a priest. Until that moment, in fact, he had avoided receiving ordination from a Bishop in dissent with the Pope. Rupert teaches us that when controversies arise in the Church the reference to the Petrine ministry guarantees fidelity to sound doctrine and is a source of serenity and inner freedom. After the dispute with Otbert Rupert was obliged to leave his monastery again twice. In 1116 his adversaries even wanted to take him to court. Although he was acquitted of every accusation, Rupert preferred to go for a while to Siegburg; but since on his return to the monastery in Liège the disputes had not yet ceased, he decided to settle definitively in Germany. In 1120 he was appointed Abbot of Deutz where, except for making a pilgrimage to Rome in 1124, he lived until 1129, the year of his death.

A fertile writer, Rupert left numerous works, still today of great interest because he played an active part in various important theological discussions of his time. For example, he intervened with determination in the Eucharistic controversy, which in 1077 led to his condemnation by Berengarius of Tours. Berengarius had given a reductive interpretation of Christ's presence in the Sacrament of the Eucharist, describing it as merely symbolic. In the language of the Church the term "transubstantiation" was as yet unknown but Rupert, at times with daring words, made himself a staunch supporter of the

Eucharistic reality and, especially in a work entitled *De divinis officiis* (*On divine offices*), purposefully asserted the continuity between the Body of the Incarnate Word of Christ and that present in the Eucharistic species of the bread and the wine.

It seems to me that at this point we must also think of our time; today too we are in danger of reappraising the Eucharistic reality, that is, of considering the Eucharist almost as a rite of communion, of socialisation alone, forgetting all too easily that the Risen Christ is really present in the Eucharist with his Risen Body which is placed in our hands *to draw us out* of ourselves, *to incorporate us* into his immortal body and thereby *lead us* to new life. This great mystery that the Lord is present in his full reality in the Eucharistic species is a mystery to be adored and loved ever anew! I would like here to quote the words of the *Catechism of the Catholic Church* which bear the fruit of 2,000 years of meditation on the faith and theological reflection: "The mode of Christ's presence under the Eucharistic species is unique and incomparable. In the most blessed sacrament of the Eucharist: the Body and Blood, together with the soul and divinity, of our Lord Jesus Christ is truly, really, and substantially contained. It is a substantial presence by which Christ, God and man, makes himself wholly and entirely present by the Eucharistic species of the bread the wine" (cf. n. *CCC* 1374). Rupert too contributed with his reflections to this precise formulation.

Another controversy in which the Abbot of Deutz was involved concerns the problem of the reconciliation of God's goodness and omnipotence with the existence of evil. If God is omnipotent and good, how is it possible to explain the reality of evil? Rupert, in fact, reacted to the position assumed by the teachers of the theological school of Laon, who, with a series of philosophical arguments, distinguished in God's will the "to approve" and the "to permit", concluding that God permits evil without approving it and hence without desiring it. Rupert, on the other hand, renounces the use of philosophy, which he deems inadequate for addressing such a great problem, and remains simply faithful to the biblical narration. He starts with the goodness of God, with the truth that God is supremely good and cannot desire anything but good. Thus he identifies the origin of evil in the human being himself and in the erroneous use of human freedom. When Rupert addresses this topic he writes pages filled with religious inspiration to praise the Father's infinite mercy, God's patience with the sinful human being and his kindness to him.

Like other medieval theologians, Rupert too wondered why the Word of God, the Son of God, was made man. Some answered by explaining the Incarnation of the Word by the urgent need to atone for human sin. Rupert, on the other hand, with a Christocentric vision of salvation history, broadens the perspective, and in a work entitled *The Glorification of the Trinity*, sustains the position that the Incarnation, the central event of the whole of history, was planned from eternity, even independently of human sin, so that the whole creation might praise God the Father and love him as one family gathered round Christ, the Son of God. Then he saw in the pregnant woman of the Apocalypse the entire history of humanity which is oriented to Christ, just as conception is oriented to birth, a perspective that was to be developed by other thinkers and enhanced by contemporary theology, which says that the whole history of the world and of humanity is a conception oriented to the birth of Christ. Christ is always the centre of the exegetic explanations

The Virgin of Dom Rupert, from the Abbey of St Lawrence in Liege,
Department of religious Art, Grand Curtius, Liege

PORTA·HEC·CLAVSA·ERIT

provided by Rupert in his commentaries on the Books of the Bible, to which he dedicated himself with great diligence and passion. Thus, he rediscovers a wonderful unity in all the events of the history of salvation, from the creation until the final consummation of time: "All Scripture", he says, "is one book, which aspires to the same end (the divine Word); which comes from one God and was written by one Spirit" (*De glorificatione Trinitatis et procesione Sancti Spiritus* I, V, PL 169, 18).

In the interpretation of the Bible, Rupert did not limit himself to repeating the teaching of the Fathers, but shows an originality of his own. For example, he is the first writer to have identified the bride in the *Song of Song*s with Mary Most Holy. His commentary on this book of Scripture has thus turned out to be a sort of Mariological *summa*, in which he presents Mary's privileges and excellent virtues. In one of the most inspired passages of his commentary Rupert writes: "O most beloved among the beloved, Virgin of virgins, what does your beloved Son so praise in you that the whole choir of angels exalts? What they praise is your simplicity, purity, innocence, doctrine, modesty, humility, integrity of mind and body, that is, your incorrupt virginity" (*In Canticum Canticorum* 4, 1-6, *CCL* 26, pp. 69-70). The Marian interpretation of Rupert's *Canticum* is a felicitous example of harmony between liturgy and theology. In fact, various passages of this Book of the Bible were already used in liturgical celebrations on Marian feasts.

Rupert, furthermore, was careful to insert his Mariological doctrine into that ecclesiological doctrine. That is to say, he saw in Mary Most Holy the holiest part of the whole Church. For this reason my venerable Predecessor, Pope Paul VI, in his Discourse for the closure of the third session of the Second Vatican Council, in solemnly pronouncing Mary Mother of the Church, even cited a proposal taken from Rupert's works, which describes Mary as *portio maxima, portio optima* the most sublime part, the very best part of the Church (*cfr. In Apocalypsem* 1. 7, *PL* 169, 1043).

From these rapid allusions we realise that Rupert was a fervent theologian endowed with great depth. Like all the representatives of monastic theology, he was able to combine rational study of the mysteries of faith with prayer and contemplation, which he considered the summit of all knowledge of God. He himself sometimes speaks of his mystical experiences, such as when he confides his ineffable joy at having perceived the Lord's presence: "in that brief moment", he says, "I experienced how true what he himself says is. Learn from me for I am meek and humble of heart" (*De gloria et honore Filii hominis. Super Matthaeum* 12, *PL* 168, 1601). We too, each one of us in our own way, can encounter the Lord Jesus who ceaselessly accompanies us on our way, making himself present in the Eucharistic Bread and in his Word for our salvation.

Onques le commun
salut est qui garde et
deffent touz ensemble
et chascun par soy. et
ce est forte vertu et han
tier sauete de vie. car il nest rien a

John of Salisbury

John of Salisbury belonged to one of the most important schools of philosophy and theology of the Middle Ages, that of the Cathedral of Chartres in France. Like the theologians of whom I have spoken in the past few weeks, John too helps us understand that faith, in harmony with the just aspirations of reason, impels thought toward the revealed truth in which is found the true good of the human being.

John was born in Salisbury, England, between 1100 and 1120. In reading his works, and especially the large collection of his letters, we learn about the most important events in his life. For about 12 years, from 1136 to 1148, he devoted himself to study, attending the best schools of his day where he heard the lectures of famous teachers. He went to Paris and then to Chartres, the environment that made the greatest impression on his formation and from which he assimilated his great cultural openness, his interest in speculative problems and his appreciation of literature. As often happened in that time, the most brilliant students were chosen by prelates and sovereigns to be their close collaborators. This also happened to John of

Music lesson, miniature from *Polycratius* by John of Salisbury, Ms. Fr. 24287, fol. 73v, Bibliothèque nationale de France, Paris

Salisbury, who was introduced to Theobald, Archbishop of Canterbury the Primatial See of England by a great friend of his, Bernard of Clairvaux. Theobald was glad to welcome John among his clergy. For 11 years, from 1150 to 1161, John was the secretary and chaplain of the elderly Archbishop. With unflagging zeal he continued to devote himself to study; he carried out an intense diplomatic activity, going to Italy ten times for the explicit purpose of fostering relations between the Kingdom and Church of England and the Roman Pontiff. Among other things, the Pope in those years was Adrian IV, an Englishman who was a close friend of John of Salisbury. In the years following Adrian IV's death, in 1159, a situation of serious tension arose in England, between the Church and the Kingdom. In fact, King Henry II wished to impose his authority on the internal life of the Church, curtailing her freedom. This stance provoked John of Salisbury to react and, in particular, prompted the valiant resistence of St Thomas Becket, Theobald's successor on the episcopal throne of Canterbury, who for this reason was exiled to France. John of Salisbury accompanied him and remained in his service, working ceaselessly for reconciliation. In 1170, when both John and Thomas Becket had returned to England, Thomas was attacked and murdered in his cathedral. He died a martyr and was immediately venerated as such by the people. John continued to serve faithfully the successor of Thomas as well, until he was appointed Bishop of Chartres where he lived from 1176 until 1180, the year of his death.

I would like to point out two of John of Salisbury's works that are considered his masterpieces, bearing elegant Greek titles: *Metalogicon* (*In Defence of Logic*), and *Policraticus* (*The Man of Government*). In the first of these works, not without that fine irony that is a feature of many scholars, he rejects the position of those who had a reductionist conception of culture, which they saw as empty eloquence and vain words. John, on the contrary, praises culture, authentic philosophy, that is, the encounter between rigorous thought and communication, effective words. He writes: "Indeed, just as eloquence that is not illuminated by reason is not only rash but blind, so wisdom that does not profit from the use of words is not only weak but in a certain way is mutilated. Indeed, although, at times, wisdom without words might serve to square the individual with his own conscience, it is of rare or little profit to society" (*Metalogicon,* 1, 1, *PL* 199, 327). This is a very timely teaching. Today, what John described as "eloquence", that is, the possibility of communicating with increasingly elaborate and widespread means, has increased enormously. Yet the need to communicate messages endowed with "wisdom", that is inspired by truth, goodness and beauty is more urgent than ever. This is a great responsibility that calls into question in particular the people who work in the multiform and complex world of culture, of communications, of the *media*. And this is a realm in which the Gospel can be proclaimed with missionary zeal.

In the *Metalogicon* John treats the problems of logic, in his day a subject of great interest, and asks himself a fundamental question: what can human reason know? To what point can it correspond with the aspiration that exists in every person, namely, to seek the truth? John of Salisbury adopts a moderate position, based on the teaching of certain treatises of Aristotle and Cicero. In his opinion human reason normally attains knowledge that is not indisputable but probable and arguable. Human knowledge this is his conclusion is imperfect, because it is subject to finiteness, to human limitations. Nevertheless it grows and is perfected, thanks to the experience and elaboration of correct and consistent reasoning, able to make connections between concepts and the reality, through discussion, exchanges and knowledge that is enriched from one generation to the next. Only in God is there perfect knowledge which is communicated to the human being, at least partially, by means of Revelation received in faith, which is why the knowledge of faith, theology, unfolds the potential of reason and makes it possible to advance with humility in the knowledge of God's mysteries.

The believer and the theologian who deepen the treasure of faith, also open themselves to a practical knowledge that guides our daily activity, in other words moral law and the exercise of the virtues. John of Salisbury writes: "God's clemency has granted us his law, which establishes what it is useful for us to know and points out to us what it is legitimate for us to know of God and what it is right to investigate... In this law, in fact, the will of God is explained and revealed so that each one of us may know what he needs to do" (*Metalogicon* 4, 41, *PL* 199, 944-945). According to John of Salisbury an immutable objective truth also exists, whose origin is in God, accessible to human reason and which concerns practical and social action. It is a natural law that must inspire human laws and political and religious authorities, so that they may promote the common good. This natural law is characterised by a property that John calls "equity", that is, the attribution to each person of his own rights. From this stem precepts that are legitimate for all peoples, and in no way can they be abrogated. This is the central thesis of *Policraticus*, the treatise of philosophy and political theology in which John of Salisbury reflects on the conditions that render government leaders' just and acceptable.

Whereas other arguments addressed in this work are linked to the historical circumstances in which it was composed, the theme of the relationship between natural law and a positive

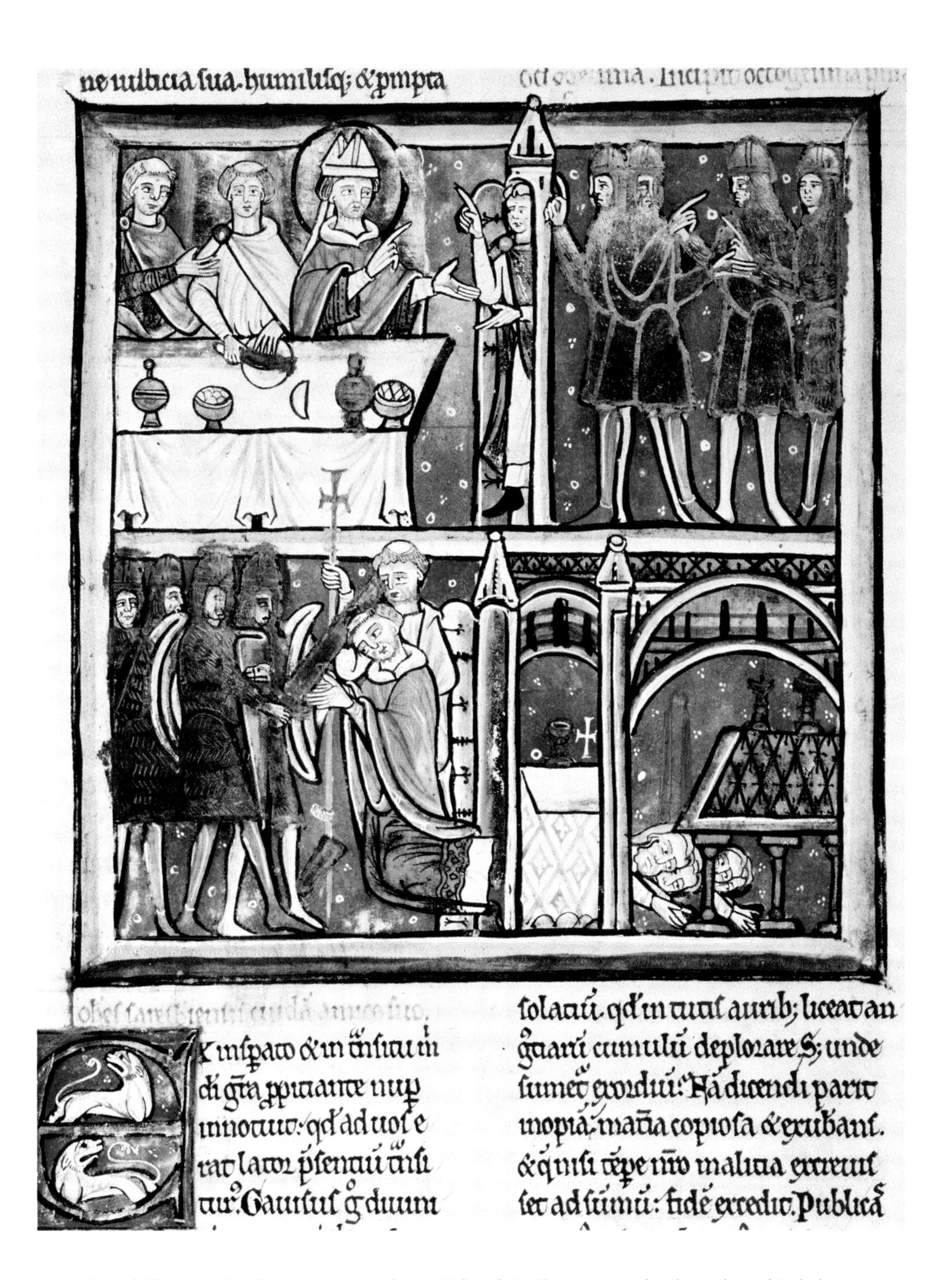

Murder of Thomas Becket, miniature from *Life of St Thomas Becket* by John of Salisbury, Cott Claud B II, fol. 341r, British Library, London

juridical order, mediated by equity, is still of great importance today. In our time, in fact, especially in some countries, we are witnessing a disturbing divergence between reason, whose task is to discover the ethical values linked to the dignity of the human person, and freedom, whose responsibility is to accept and promote them. Perhaps John of Salisbury would remind us today that the only laws in conformity with equity are those that protect the sacredness of human life and reject the licitness of abortion, euthanasia and bold genetic experimentation, those laws that respect the dignity of marriage between a man and a woman, that are inspired by a correct secularism of the State a secularism that always entails the safeguard of religious freedom and that pursue subsidiarity and solidarity at both the national and the international level. If this were not so, what John of Salisbury terms the "tyranny of princes", or as we would say, "the dictatorship of relativism" would end by coming to power, a relativism, as I recalled a few years ago, "which does not recognise anything as definitive and whose ultimate goal consists solely of one's own ego and desires" (Cardinal Joseph Ratzinger, Dean of the College of Cardinals, *Homily, Mass for the Election of the Roman Pontiff,* 18 April 2005).

In my most recent Encyclical, *Caritas in Veritate*, in addressing people of good will who strive to ensure that social and political action are never separated from the objective truth about man and his dignity, I wrote: "Truth, and the love which it reveals, cannot be produced: they can only be received as a gift. Their ultimate source is not, and cannot be, mankind, but only God, who is himself Truth and Love. This principle is extremely important for society and for development, since neither can be a purely human product; the vocation to development on the part of individuals and peoples is not based simply on human choice, but is an intrinsic part of a plan that is prior to us and constitutes for all of us a duty to be freely accepted" (n. 52). We must seek and welcome this plan that precedes us, this truth of being, so that justice may be born, but we may find it and welcome it only with a heart, a will and a reason purified in the light of God.

PIERRE LOMBARD dict le Mre des Sentences
Evesque de Paris . mourut lan . 1164 .

Peter Lombard

In this chapter I would like to speak of Peter Lombard: he was a theologian who lived in the 12th century and enjoyed great fame because one of his works, entitled the *Sentences*, was used as a theological manual for many centuries.

So who was Peter Lombard? Although the information on his life is scarce it is possible to reconstruct the essential lines of his biography. He was born beween the 11th and 12th centuries near Novara, in Northern Italy, in a region that once belonged to the Lombards. For this very reason he was nicknamed "the Lombard". He belonged to a modest family, as we may deduce from the letter of introduction that Bernard of Clairvaux wrote to Gilduin, Superior of the Abbey of Saint-Victor in Paris, asking him to give free accomodation to Peter who wanted to go to that city in order to study. In fact, even in the Middle Ages not only nobles or the rich might study and acquire important roles in ecclesial and social life but also people of humble origin such as, for example, Gregory VII, the Pope who stood up to the Emperor Henry VI, or Maurice of Sully, the Archbishop of Paris who

Peter Lombard, illustration from *Les Vrais portraits et vies des homes illustres* by André Thevet, Bibliothèque nationale de France, Paris commissioned the building of Notre-Dame and who was the son of a poor peasant.

Peter Lombard began his studies in Bologna and then went to Rheims and lastly to Paris. From 1140 he taught at the prestigious school of Notre-Dame. Esteemed and appreciated as a theologian, eight years later he was charged by Pope Eugene III to examine the doctrine of Gilbert de la Porrée, that was giving rise to numerous discussions, because it was held to be not wholly orthodox. Having become a priest, he was appointed Bishop of Paris in 1159, a year before his death in 1160.

Like all theology teachers of his time, Peter also wrote discourses and commentaries on Sacred Scripture. His masterpiece, however, consists of the four Books of the *Sentences*. This is a text which came into being for didactic purposes. According to the theological method in use in those times, it was necessary first of all to know, study and comment on the thought of the Fathers of the Church and of the other writers deemed authoritative. Peter therefore collected a very considerable amount of documentation, which consisted mainly of the teachings of the great Latin Fathers, especially St Augustine, and was open to the contribution of contemporary theologians. Among other things, he also used an encyclopedia of Greek theology which had only recently become known to the West: *The Orthodox faith*, composed by St John Damascene. The great merit of Peter Lombard is to have organised all the material that he had collected and chosen with care, in a systematic and harmonious framework. In fact one of the features of theology is to organise the patrimony of faith in a unitive and orderly way. Thus he distributed the sentences, that is, the Patristic sources on various arguments, in four books. In the first book he addresses God and the Trinitarian mystery; in the second, the work of the Creation, sin and Grace; in the third, the Mystery of the Incarnation and the work of Redemption with an extensive exposition on the virtues. The fourth book is dedicated to the sacraments and to the last realities, those of eternal life, or *Novissimi*. The overall view presented includes almost all the truths of the Catholic faith. The concise, clear vision and clear, orderly schematic and ever consistent presentation explain the extraordinary success of Peter Lombard's *Sentences*. They enabled students to learn reliably and gave the educators and teachers who used them plenty of room for acquiring deeper knowledge. A Franciscan theologian, Alexandre of Hales, of the next generation, introduced into the *Sentences* a division that facilitated their study and consultation. Even the greatest of the 13th-century theologians, Albert the Great, Bonaventure of Bagnoregio and Thomas Aquinas began their academic activity by commenting on the four books of Peter Lombard's *Sentences*, enriching them with their reflections. Lombard's text was the book in use at all schools of theology until the 16th century.

I would like to emphasise how the organic presentation of faith is an indispensable requirement. In fact, the individual truths of faith illuminate each other and, in their total and unitive vision appears the harmony of God's plan of salvation and the centrality of the Mystery of Christ. After the example of Peter Lombard, I invite all theologians and priests always to keep in mind the whole vision of the Christian doctrine, to counter today's risks of fragmentation and the debasement of the single truths. The *Catechism of the Catholic Church*, as well as the *Compendium* of this same Catechism, offer us exactly this full picture of Christian Revelation, to be accepted with faith and gratitude. However I would like to encourage the individual faithful and the Christian communities to make the most of these instruments to know and to deepen the content of our faith. It will thus appear to us as a marvellous symphony that speaks to us of God and of his love and asks of us firm adherence and an active response.

To get an idea of the interest that the reading of Peter Lombard's *Sentences* still inspires today I propose two examples. Inspired by St Augustine's Commentary on the Book of Genesis, Peter wonders why woman was created from man's rib and not from his head or his feet. And Peter explains: "She was formed neither as a dominator nor a slave of man but rather as his companion" (*Sentences* 3, 18, 3). Then, still on the basis of the Patristic teaching he adds: "The mystery of Christ and of the Church is represented in this act. Just as, in fact, woman was formed from Adam's rib while he slept, so the Church was born from the sacraments that began to flow from the side of Christ, asleep on the Cross, that is, from the blood and water with which we are redeemed from sin and cleansed of guilt" (*Sentences* 3, 18, 4). These are profound reflections that still apply today when the theology and spirituality of Christian marriage have considerably deepened the analogy with the spousal relationship of Christ and his Church.

In another passage in one of his principal works, Peter Lombard, treating the merits of Christ, asks himself: "Why, then does [Christ] wish to suffer and die, if his virtues were sufficient to obtain for himself all the merits?". His answer is incisive and effective: "For you, not for himself!". He then continues with another question and another answer, which seem to reproduce the discussions that went on during the lessons of medieval theology teachers: "And in what sense did he suffer and die for me? So that his Passion and his death might be an example and cause for you. An example of virtue and humility, a cause of glory and freedom; an example given by God, obedient unto death; a cause of your liberation and your beatitude" (*Sentences* 3, 18, 5).

Among the most important contributions offered by Peter Lombard to the history of theology, I would like to recall his treatise on the sacraments, of which he gave what I would call a definitive definition: "precisely what is a sign of God's grace and a visible form of invisible grace, in such a way that it bears its image and is its cause is called a sacrament in the proper sense" (4, 1, 4). With this definition Peter Lombard grasps the essence of the sacraments: they are a cause of grace, they are truly able to communicate divine life. Successive theologians never again departed from this vision and were also to use the distinction between the material and the formal element introduced by the "Master of the Sentences", as Peter Lombard was known. The material element is the tangible visible reality, the formal element consists of the words spoken by the minister. For a complete and valid celebration of the sacraments both are essential: matter, the reality with which the Lord visibly touches us and the word that conveys the spiritual significance. In Baptism, for example, the material element is the water that is poured on the head of the child and the formal element is the formula: "I baptise you in the name of the Father, of the Son and of the Holy Spirit". Peter the Lombard, moreover, explained that the sacraments alone objectively transmit divine grace and they are seven: Baptism, the Eucharist, Penance, the Unction of the sick, Orders and Matrimony (cf. *Sentences* 4, 2, 1).

It is important to recognise how precious and indispensable for every Christian is the sacramental life in which the Lord transmits this matter in the community of the Church, and touches and transforms us. As the *Catechism of the Catholic Church* says, the sacraments are "powers that come forth from the Body of Christ, which is ever-living and life-giving. They are actions of the Holy Spirit" (n. 1116). In this Year for Priests

Andrea Bonaiuti, *Triumph of St Thomas Aquinas,* detail, Santa Maria Novella, Florence

which we are celebrating I urge priests, especially ministers in charge of souls, to have an intense sacramental life themselves in the first place in order to be of help to the faithful. May the celebration of the sacraments be impressed with dignity and decorum, encourage personal recollection and community participation, the sense of God's presence and missionary zeal. The sacraments are the great treasure of the Church and it is the task of each one of us to celebrate them with spiritual profit. In them an ever amazing event touches our lives: Christ, through the visible signs, comes to us, purifies us, transforms us and makes us share in his divine friendship.

INDEX OF AUDIENCES

Entry of Peter the Venerable into school, stained glass window, Church of Saint-Jean, Sauxillanges

INDEX OF ILLUSTRATIONS

PICTURE CREDITS

Archivio Ultreya, Milan, 16

© Bayerische Staatsbibliothek München, 100

© Bibliothèque nationale de France, 38, 70, 94, 108, 116

Bildarchiv Monheim/Archivi Alinari,Firenze, 81, 82

© Bodleian Library, Oxford, 86

© British Library, London, 91

© Editoriale Jaca Book, Milano, 24

Foto Musée Jacquemart-André/Inst. De France/Scala, Firenze, 59

© Foto Scala Firenze/Heritage Images, 68

© Foto Scala, Firenze – by kind permission of Ministero Beni e Attività Culturali, 48, 50

© Foto Scala, Firenze, 35, 47, 54

cover

© Foto Scala, Firenze/Fondo Edifici di Culto – Ministero dell'Interno, 122

© Franco Cosimo Panini, 20, 62

© Liè ge, Grand Curtius, Département d'Art religieux et d'Art mosan, 105

© Photoservice Electa/Akg images, 30, 124

© Photoservice Electa/Leemage, 74-75

Raffaello Bencini/Archivi Alinari, Firenze, 6-7

© RMN (Domaine de Chantilly)/René-Gabriel Ojéda – Réunion des Musée Nationaux/
distr. Alinari, 32, 65

The Bridgeman Art Library/Archivi Alinari, Firenze, 8, 13, 44, 78, 113